Kamloops British Columbia Canada Book 3 in Colour Photos, Saving Our History One Photo at a Time

Photography by Barbara Raué
©2019

Series Name: Cruising Canada

Book 17: Kamloops Book 3

Cover photo: 868 Nicola Street, Page 41

© 2019 by Barbara Raue - All the photos in this book have been taken with my cameras. I own the rights to them.

Series Name: Cruising Canada
Saving Our History One Photo at a Time
in colour photos

Book 1-9: Winnipeg Manitoba
Book 10: Osoyoos, B.C.
Book 11: Vernon, Salmon Arm
Book 12: Kelowna
Book 13: Penticton
Book 14: Hope
Book 15-17: Kamloops

Table of Contents

Nicola Street	Page 4
Royal Avenue	Page 57
Tranquille Road	Page 60
Fortune Drive	Page 62

Kamloops is a city in south central British Columbia in Canada, located at the confluence of the two branches of the Thompson River near Kamloops Lake.

The first European explorer, David Stuart, arrived in 1811; he was sent out from Fort Astoria, a Pacific Fur Company post; he spent a winter there with the Secwepemc people. He and Alexander Ross established a post there in May 1812, "Fort Cumcloups".

The rival North West Company established another post, Fort Shuswap, nearby in the same year. The two operations were merged in 1813 when the North West Company officials in the region bought out the operations of the Pacific Fur Company. After the North West Company's forced merger with the Hudson's Bay Company in 1821, the post became known commonly as Thompson's River Post, or Fort Thompson, which over time became known as Fort Kamloops.

After the fur trade arrived in 1812, Kamloops became the crossroads for horse-drawn pack trains. In the years that followed, Kamloops' reputation as a bristling locality for trade and commerce was greatly broadened by the gold rush of the 1850s, among other things. Following the arrival of the first permanent ranchers was the railway which came through in 1893; Kamloops continued to be the resting stop for the weary travelers. Kamloops has continued to grow since then with cattle ranching, forestry and mining.

The gold rush of the 1860s and the construction of the Canadian Pacific Railway, which reached Kamloops from the West in 1883, brought further growth.

Pulp, plywood, veneer, cement, and a copper mine are industries in Kamloops. The Royal Inland Hospital is the city's largest employer. Thompson River University serves a student body of 10,000.

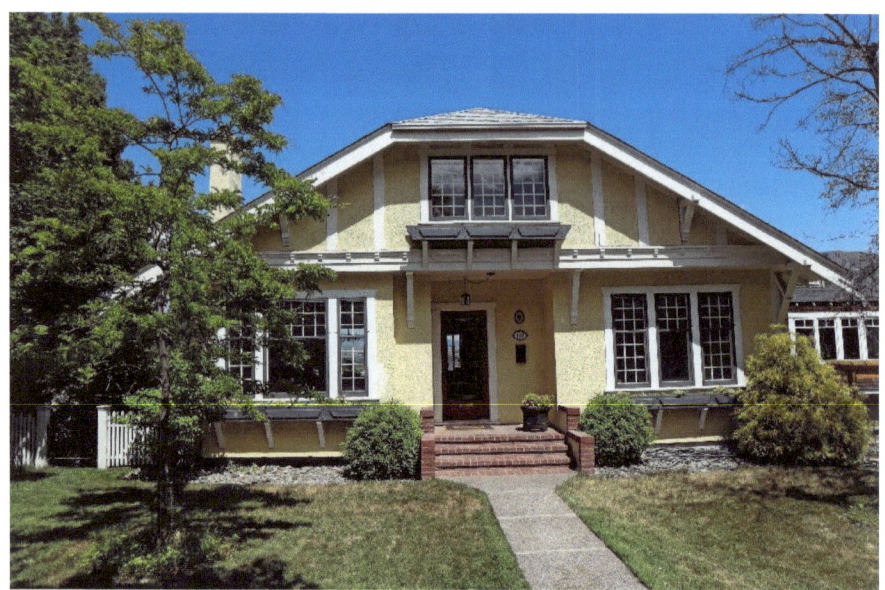

118 Nicola Street – William O. Ellis House - W.O. Ellis was a local pharmacist and active community member. He built his home on tree lined Nicola Street in 1929. It has many features typical of the Arts and Crafts style, but it is also looking forward to architectural trends popularized in the 1930s. The cream-colored stucco, green window boxes, and red steps are the original colors.

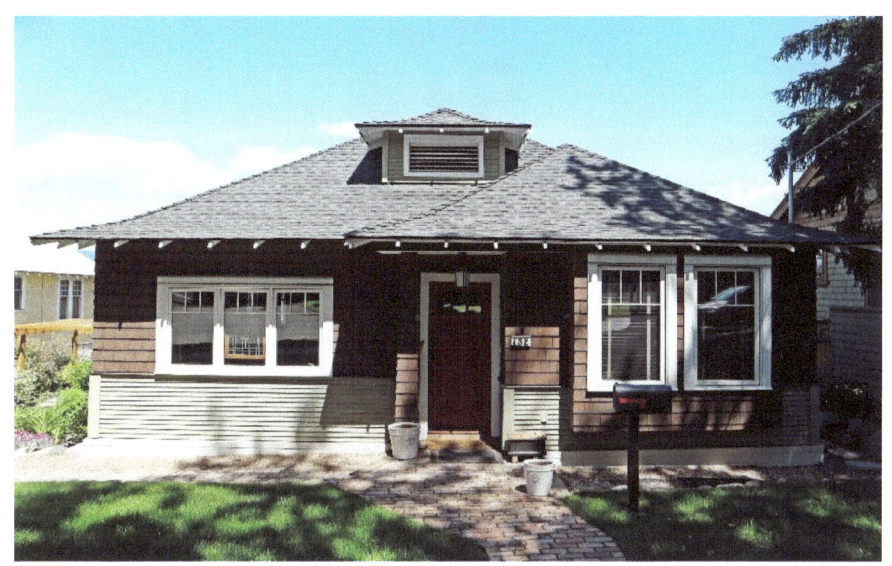

132 Nicola Street

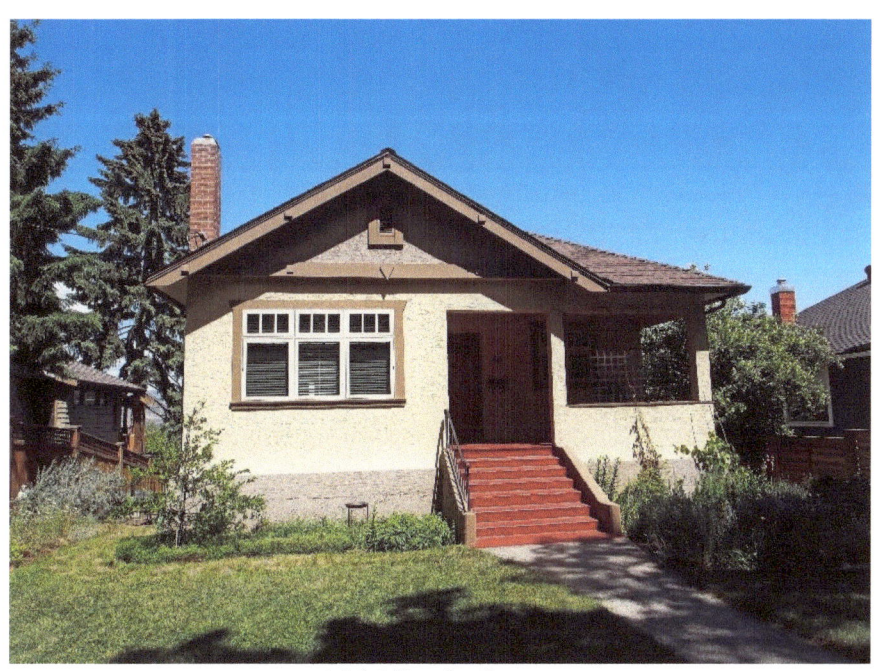

146 Nicola Street

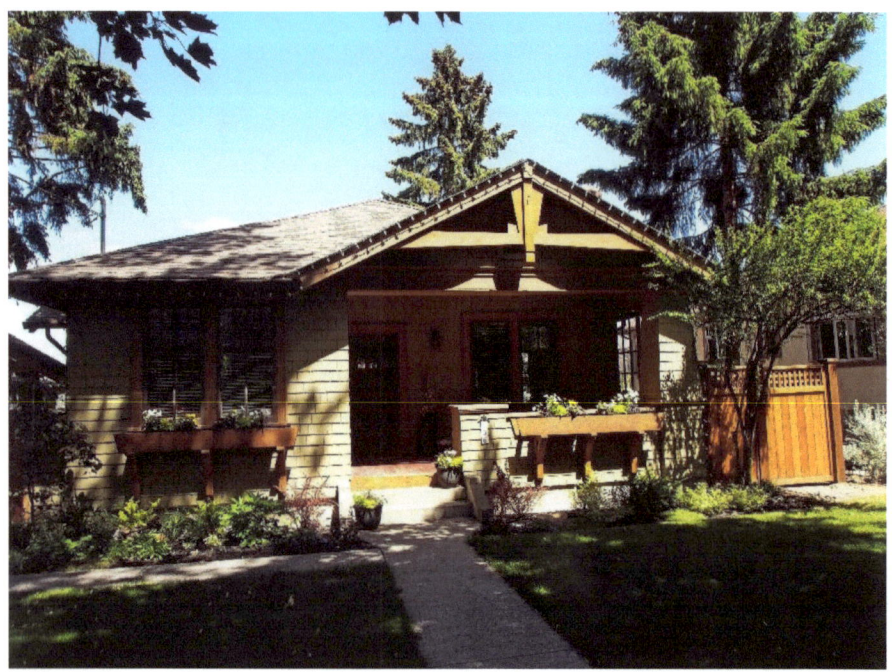

136 Nicola Street – Hamilton House - The Craftsman style that was popular in the 1920s is evident in this house built in 1923. Original features such as the cedar shingle siding, v board soffits, exposed rafter fascia, multi-pane windows and verandah have been well maintained.

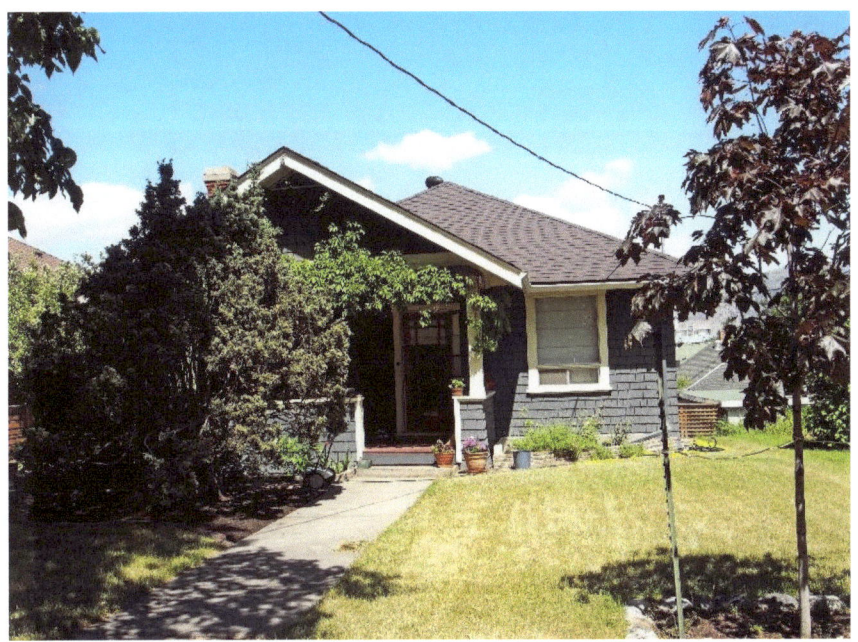

154 Nicola Street

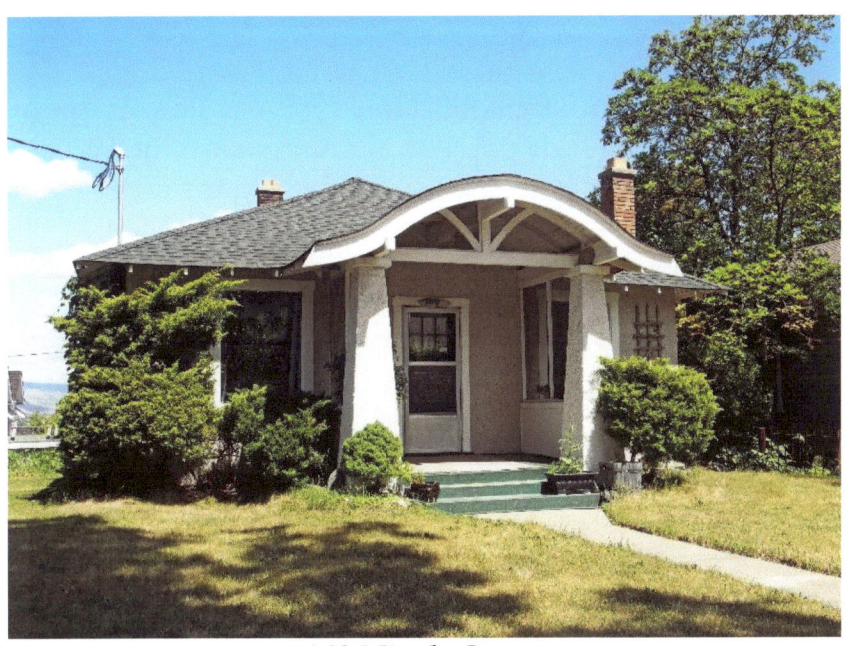

160 Nicola Street

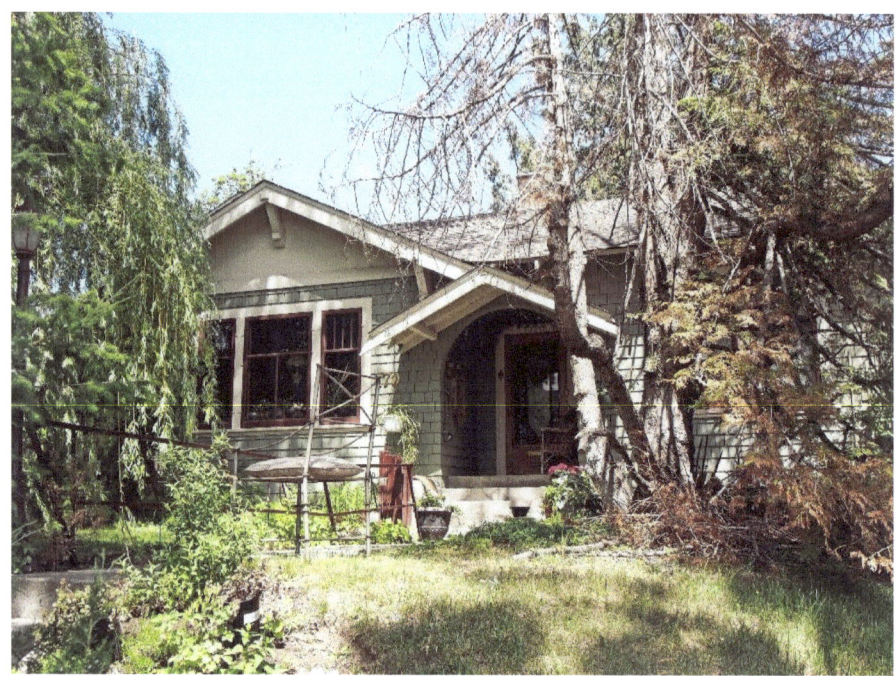

170 Nicola Street – George Ellis House is a classic example of the Arts and Crafts style popular in Kamloops in the 1920s. The house was built in 1923 and includes cedar shingle siding, and roofing, tapering verandah columns, multi-paned windows, exposed rafter ends and decorative barge boards. The garden complements the house.

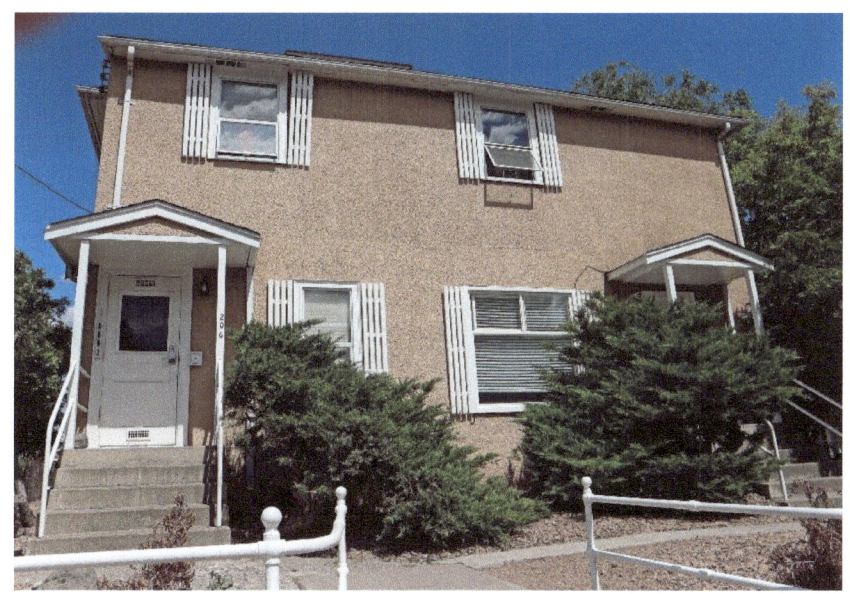

206 Nicola Street

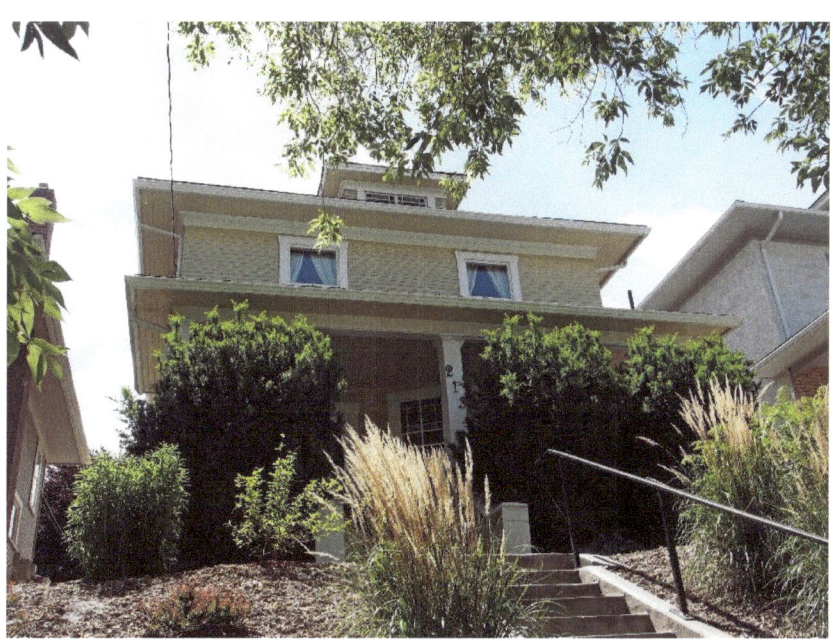

213 Nicola Street

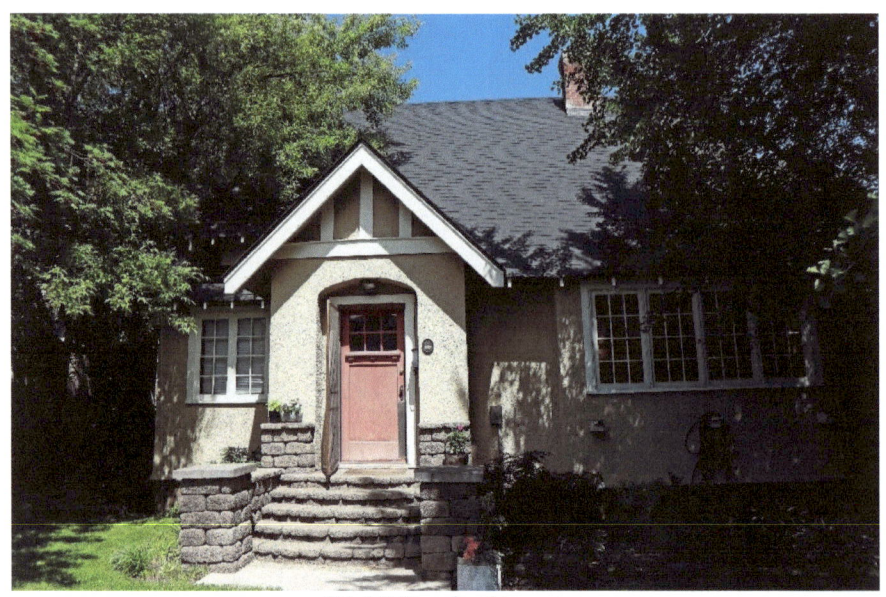

214 Nicola Street

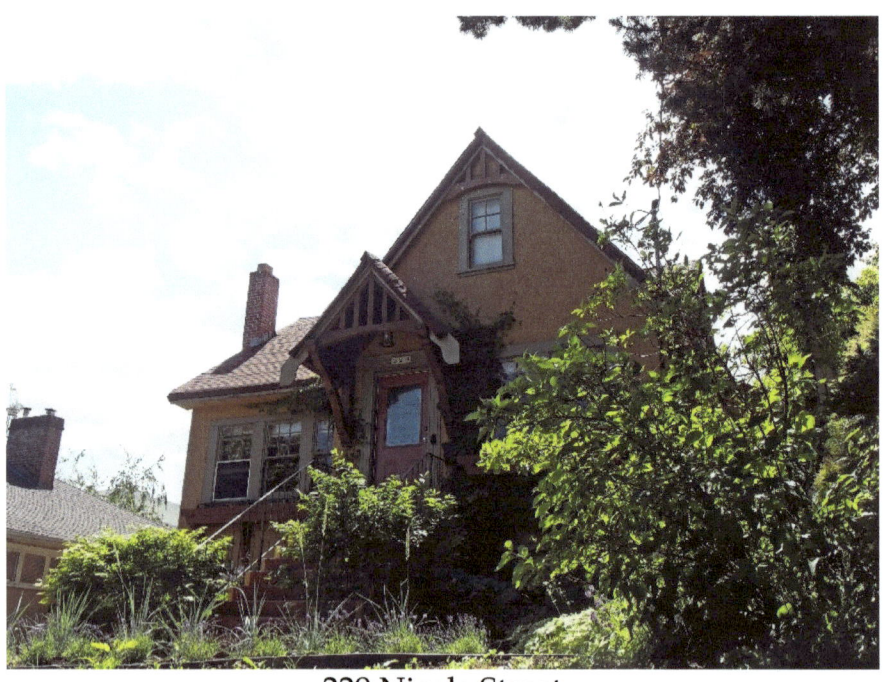

229 Nicola Street

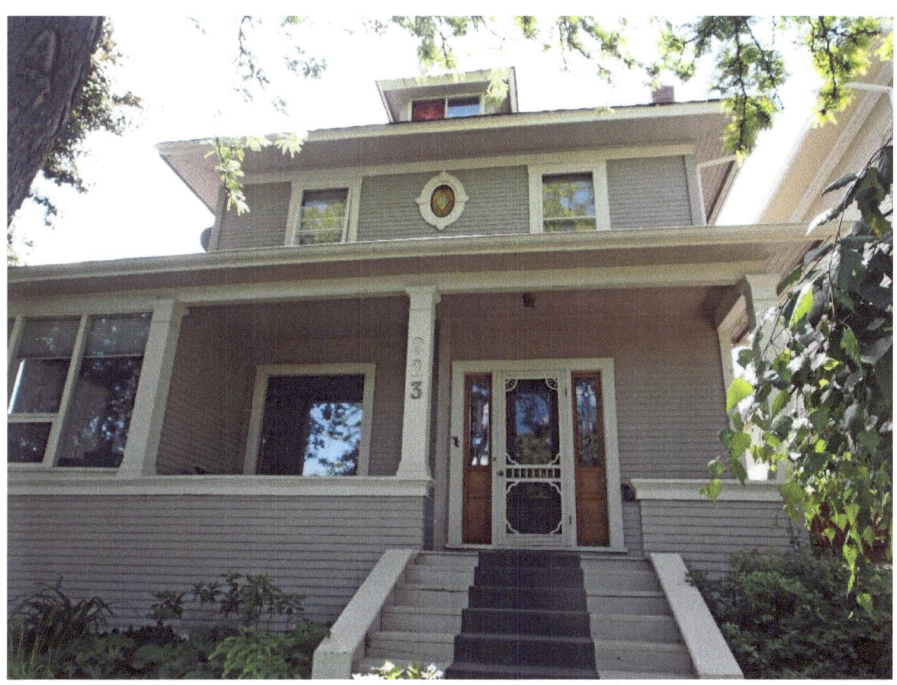

223 Nicola Street – The style of this home is typical of the 1910 period in Kamloops and is best described as anti-Victorian in sentiment. It was built in 1909. The overall shape is rectangular and right-angled. Adornment is kept to a minimum. Homes like this can be found scattered throughout Kamloops and were generally owned by small businessmen or railway officials.

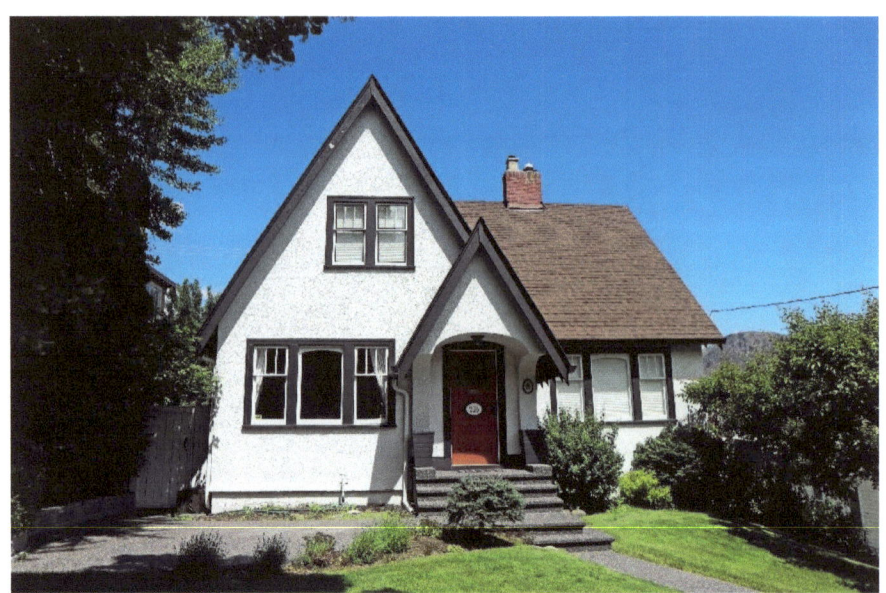

226 Nicola Street – S. B. Brooke House - This English style cottage was built in 1940 by C.N.R. Conductor Bernard Brooke (aka 'Babbling Brooke') and his wife Ruby, after their home at 1426 Lorne Street burned to the ground. Mrs. Brooke and her two children escaped into the -20°F weather at midnight with only their overcoats and nightclothes. The fire brigade's efforts were hampered by the extreme cold and a broken fire hydrant. Mr. Brooke returned home to find that his wife had narrowly escaped the flames, as the front door had jammed, making her exit difficult.

In 1942, C.N.R. Engineer, Archibald Legg and his new bride Janet Darlington purchased this home. The couple were former neighbors in the 800 block Battle Street when both became widowed. Sadly, Archibald Legg was killed in 1948, in a train wreck near Lytton, and Janet remained in the house until 1970.

The architecture of this stucco house is unique in the Kamloops area. The steep pitched, double peaks at the front of the house are repeated once at the rear. These details were labor intensive, but add greatly to the appeal of the home inside and out. This four-bedroom cottage has only one bathroom; however, an upstairs bedroom features the original built-in vanity sink. Chamber pots were probably a necessity as one of the resident families had seven children.

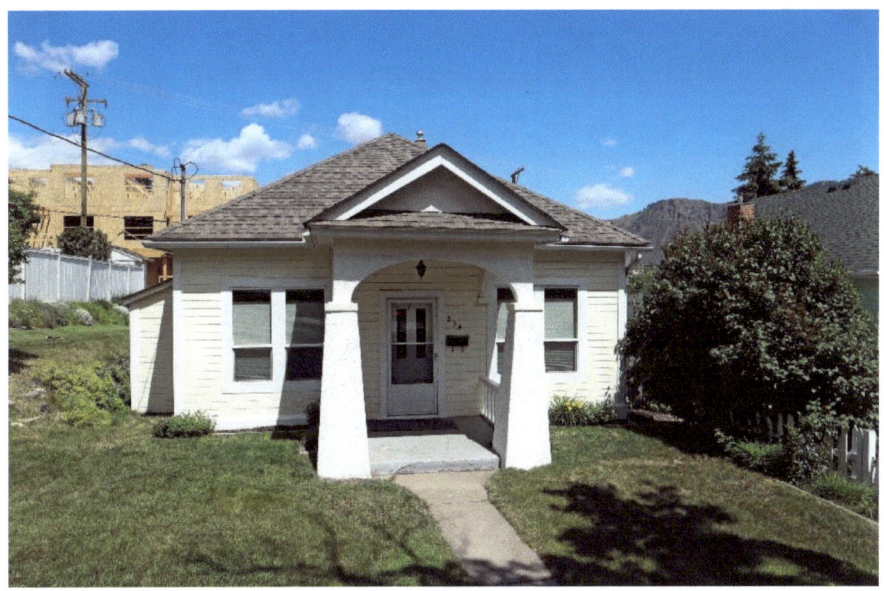

234 Nicola Street

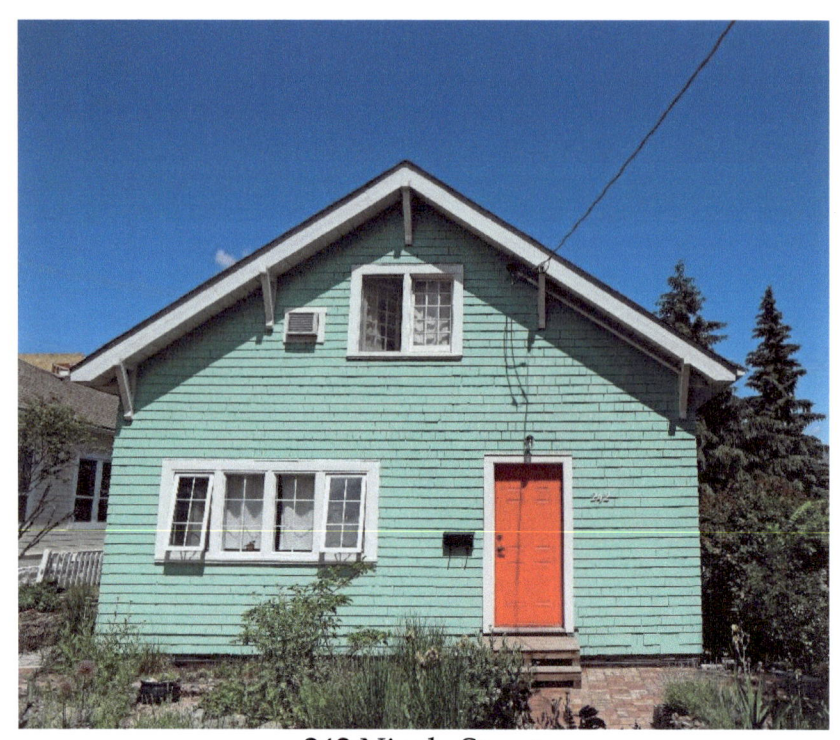
242 Nicola Street

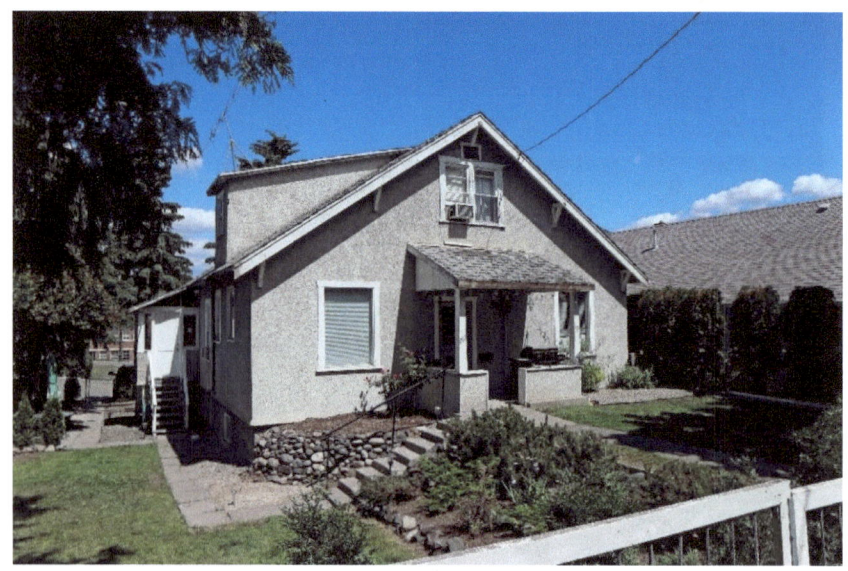
248 Nicola Street

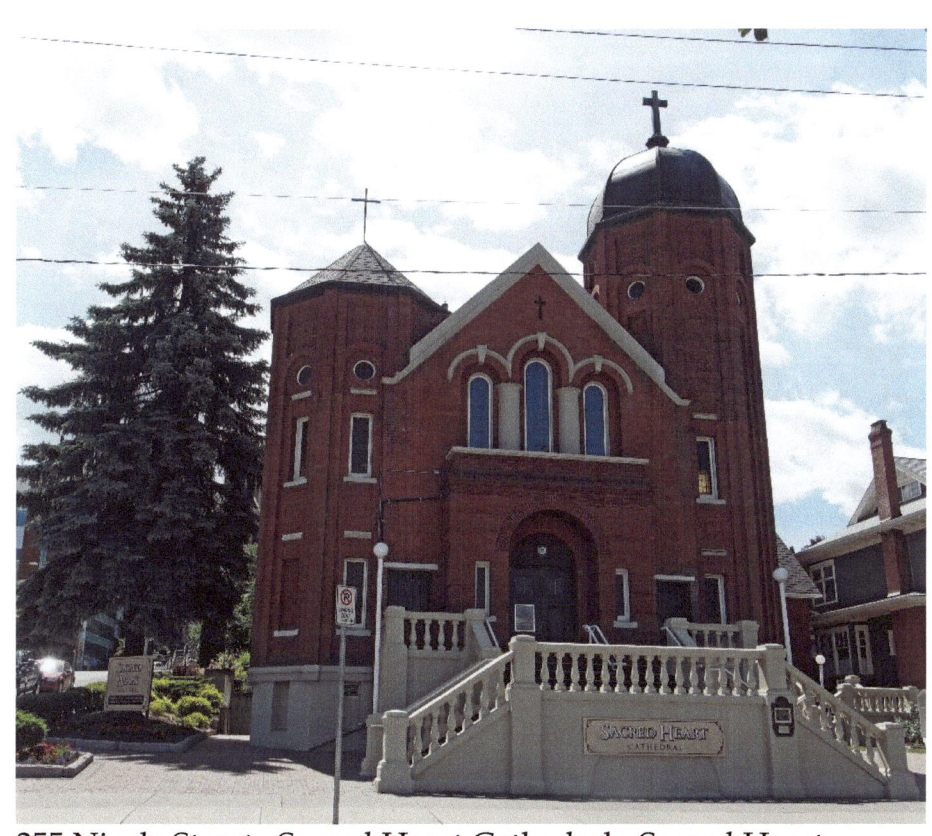

255 Nicola Street –Sacred Heart Cathedral - Sacred Heart Cathedral was built in 1921 to replace a wood frame church which had burned. Interesting architectural features include stained and leaded glass windows, red brick with white stone accents, columns, balustrade, a tower, and dome. The interior is dominated by an elaborate altar.

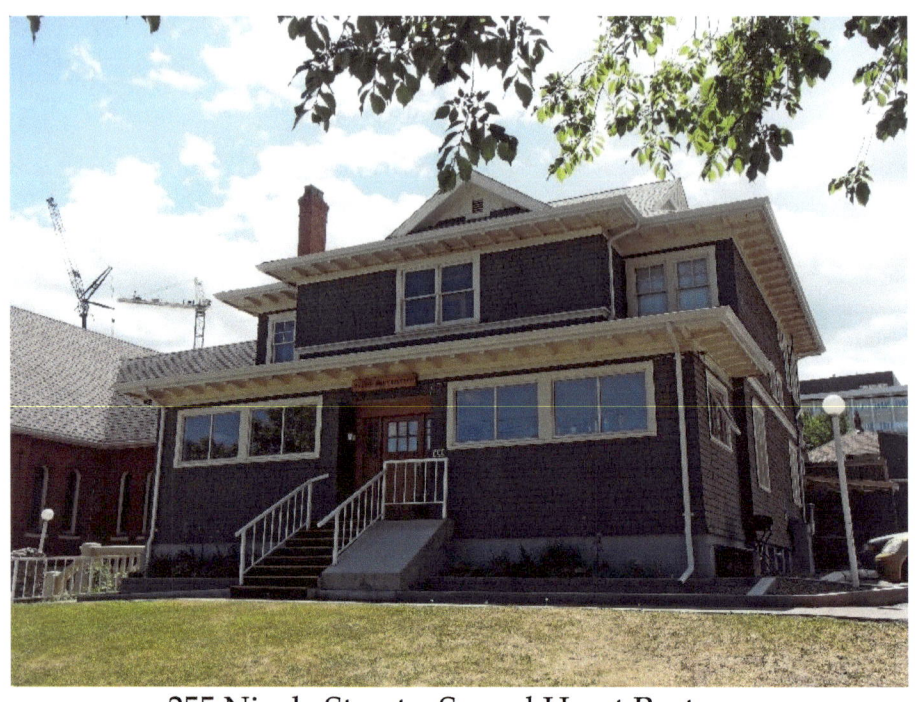

255 Nicola Street – Sacred Heart Rectory

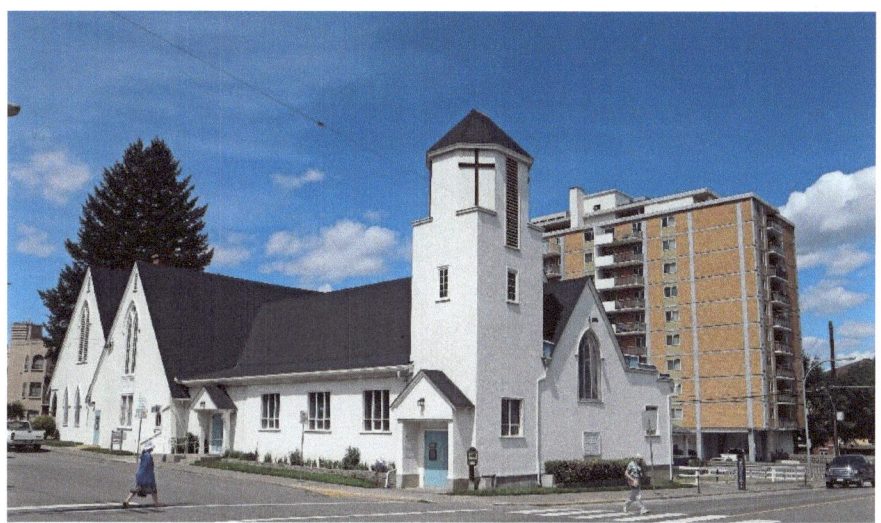

360 Nicola Street – St. Paul's Church - The Anglican parish of Kamloops built a new wood frame church, St. Paul's in 1889 in order to accommodate a growing congregation. A gale in 1890 knocked the bell tower down and it took until 1892 to build a new belfry. A fire badly damaged the floor in 1891 and it was saved by the fire brigade's quick response.

The church was both a religious and cultural center. Bishop Sillitoe on a visit to the city presented the first lantern slide show in the community. Summer picnics, Christmas parties and concerts for various celebrations were popular. In 1912 three artistic stained-glass windows made in Montreal representing Faith, Hope and Charity were installed in memory of local pioneers.

Starting in 1911 the parish discussed moving out of the crowded West Victoria area. In 1924 the church and hall were cut into sections and moved by a horse drawn six-wheel trolley to its new site at Fourth Avenue and Nicola Street where it was redesigned in a Tudor style. The original wood structures remain embedded within the existing enlarged Cathedral.

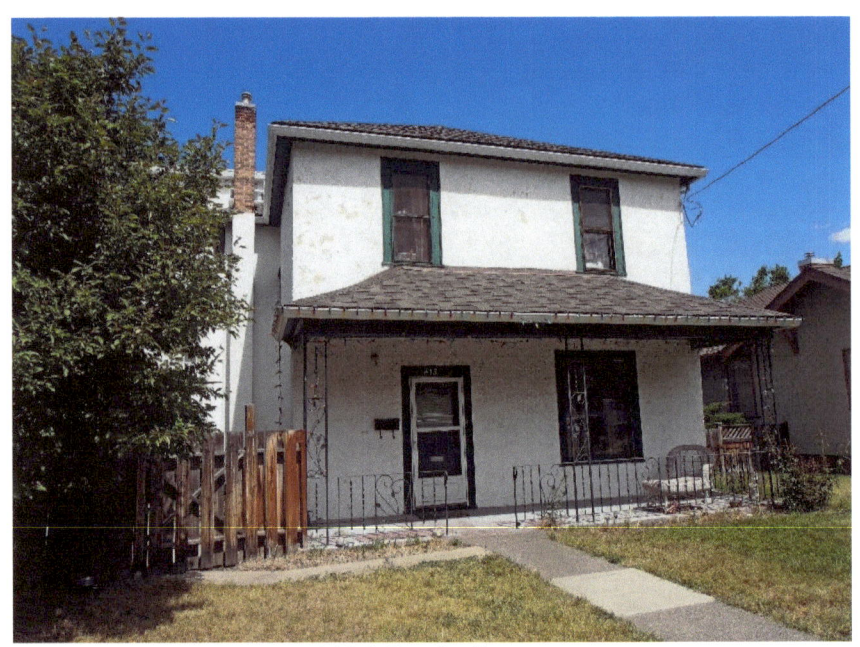

412 Nicola Street

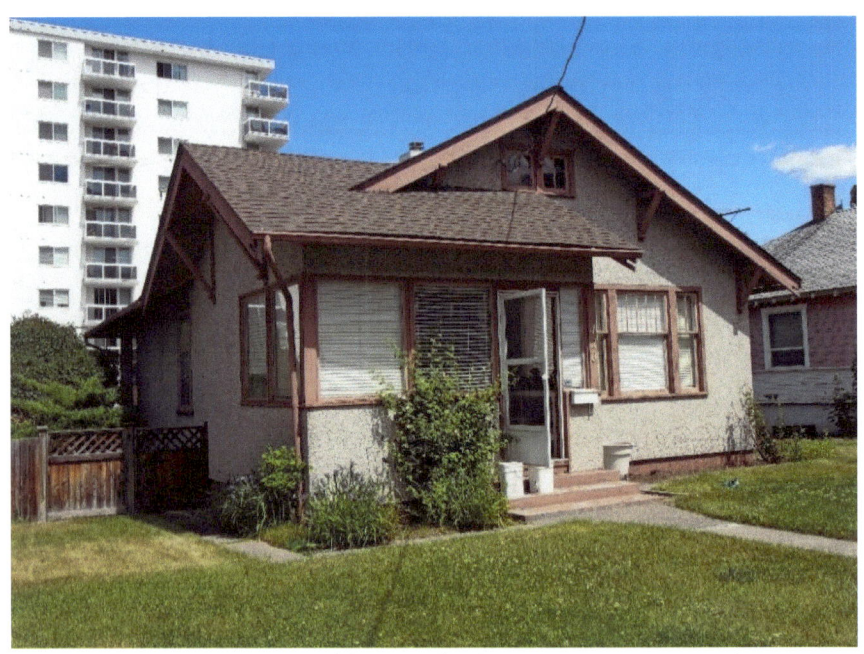

420 Nicola Street

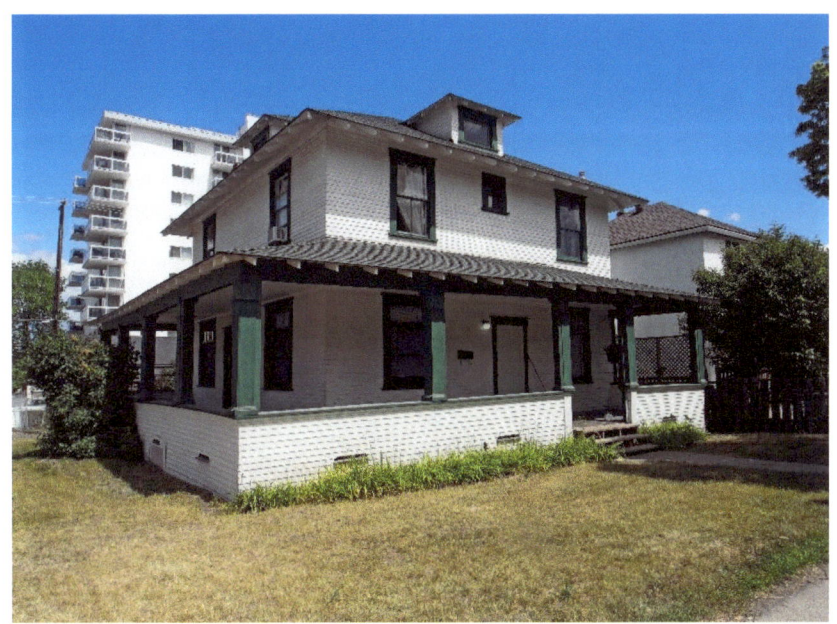

425 Nicola Street

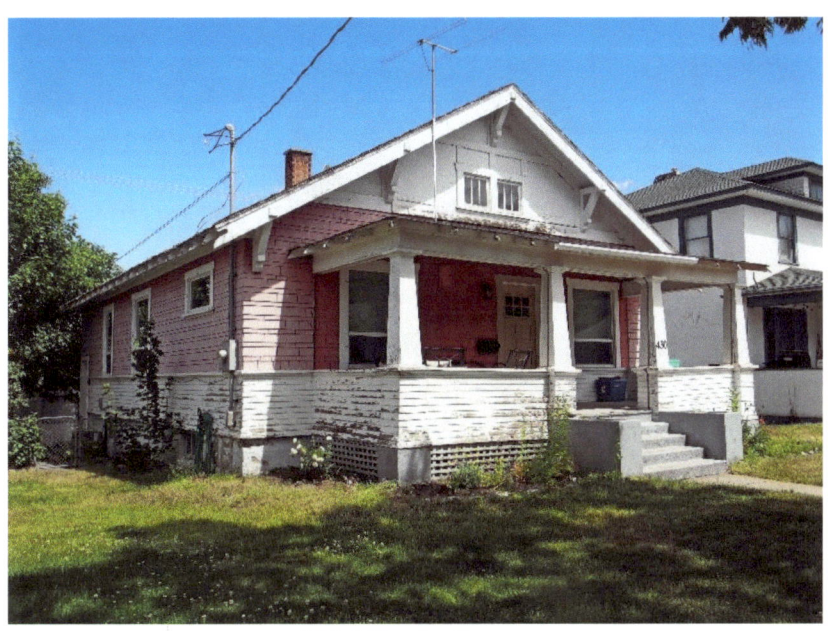

430 Nicola Street

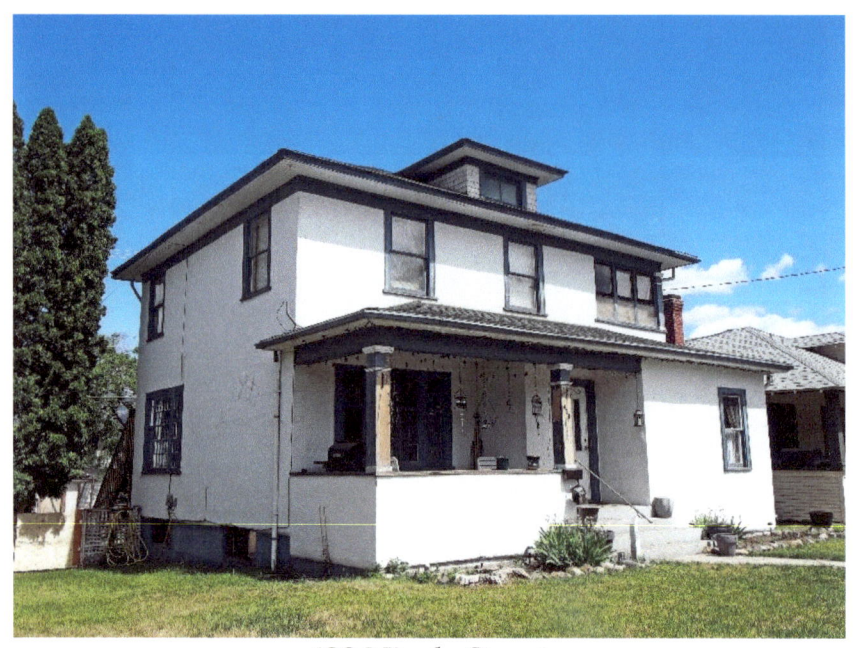

438 Nicola Street

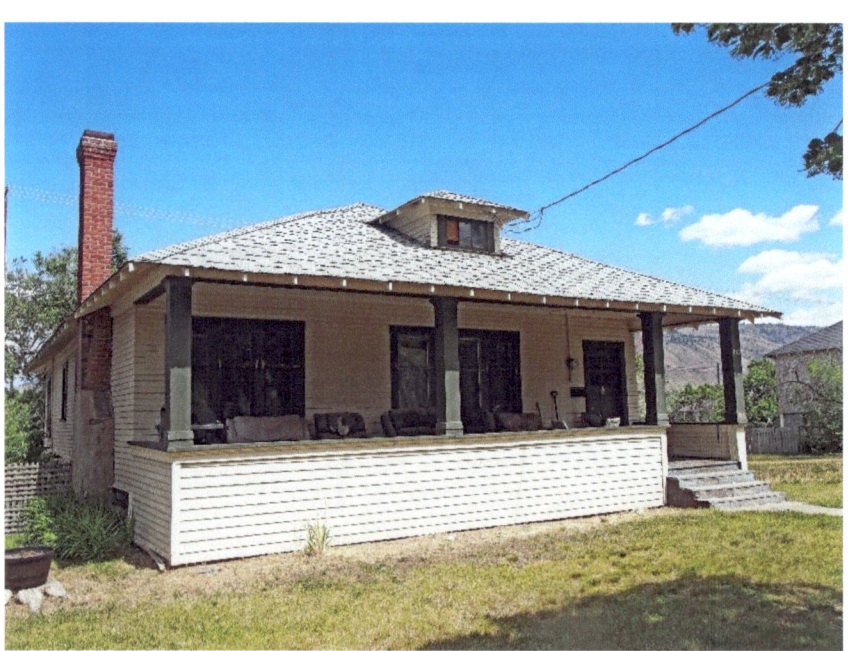

448 Nicola Street

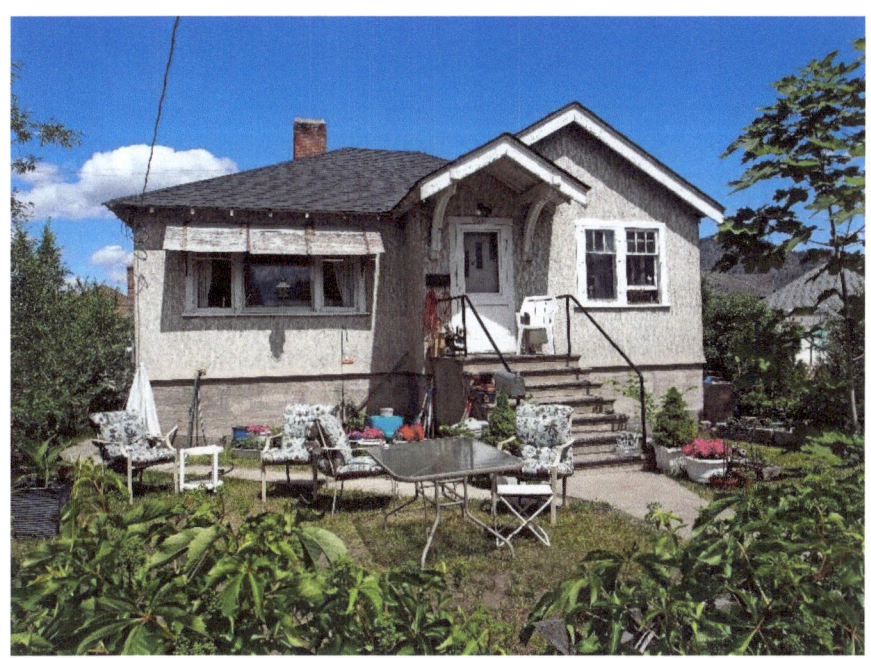

460 Nicola Street

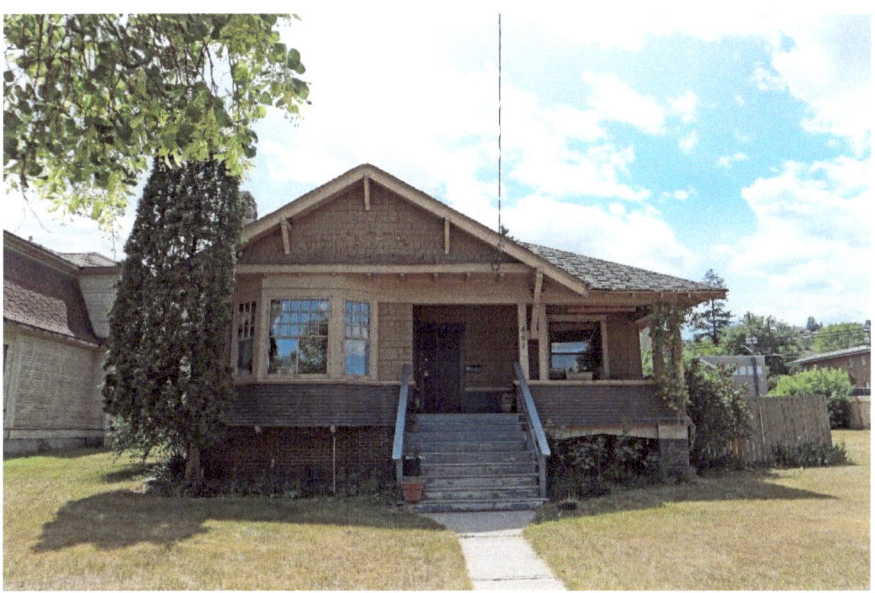

461 Nicola Street

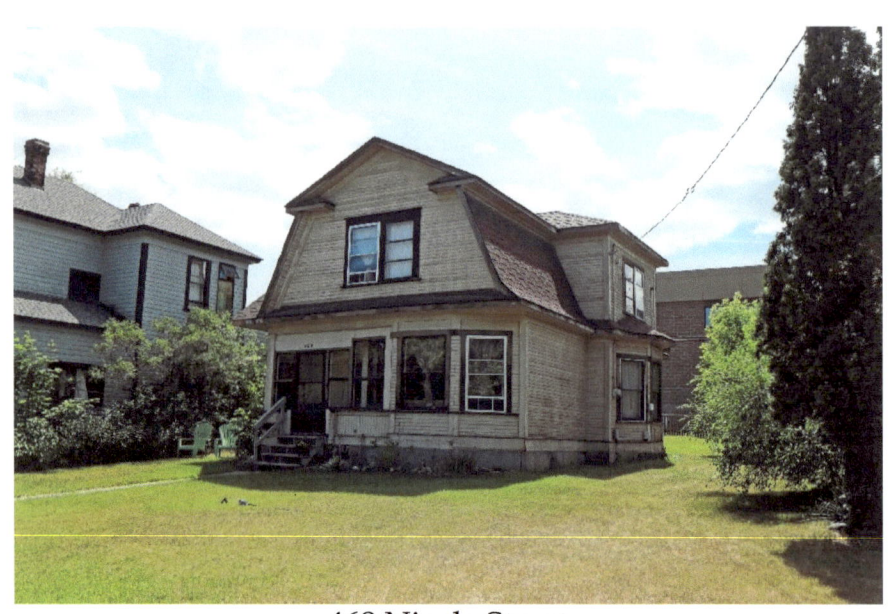

469 Nicola Street

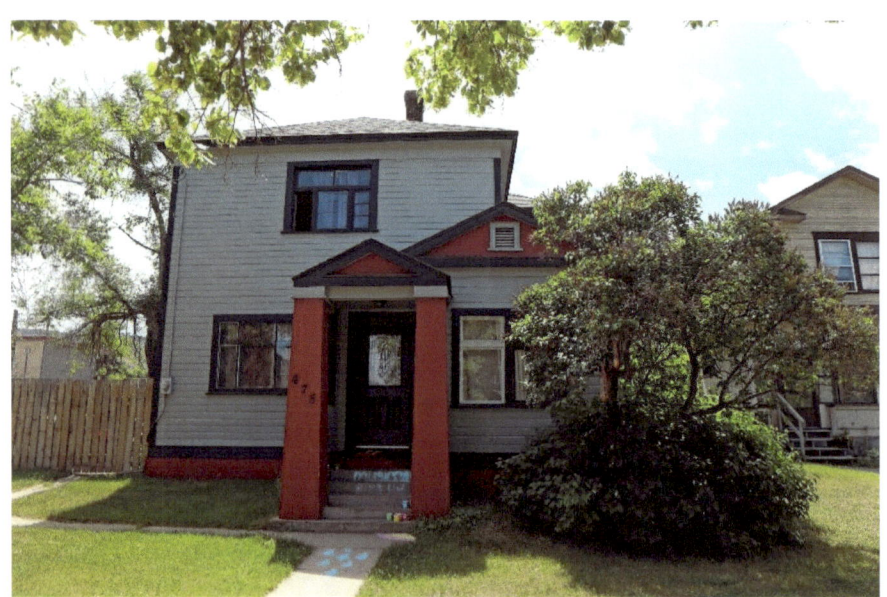

475 Nicola Street

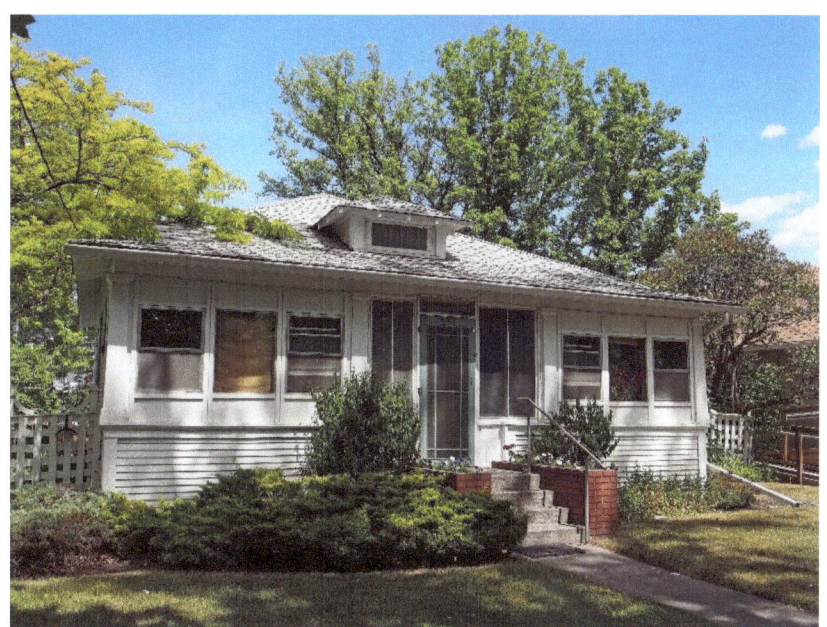

534 Nicola Street

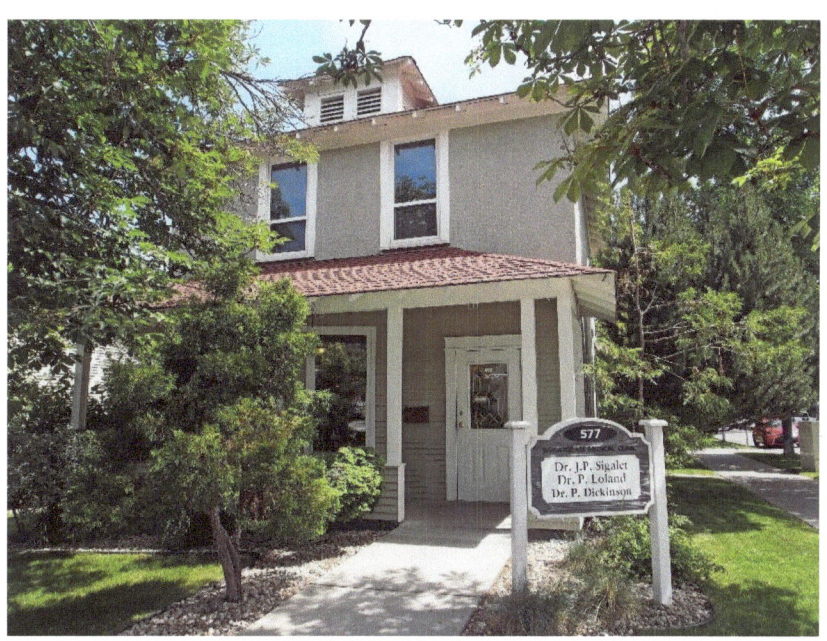

577 Nicola Street

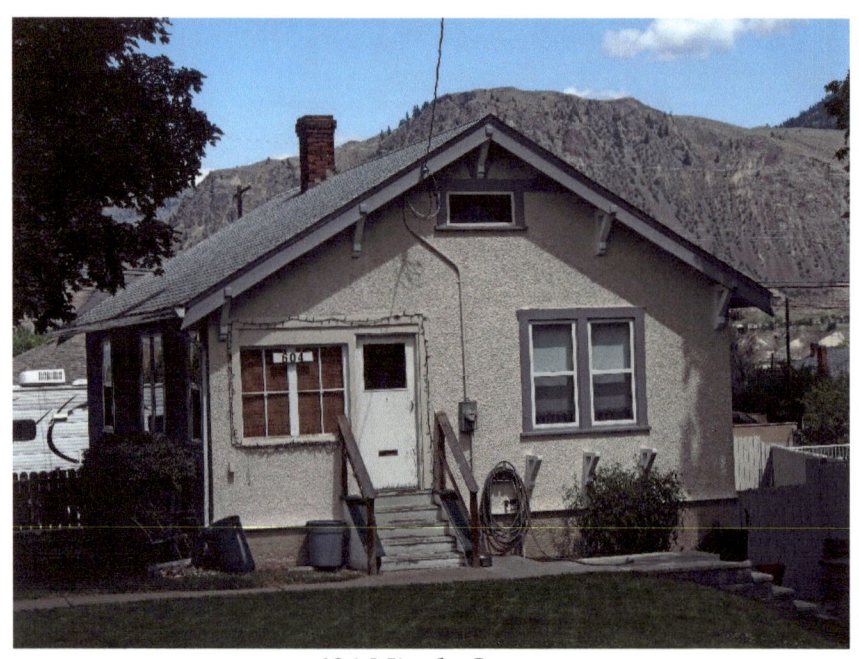
604 Nicola Street

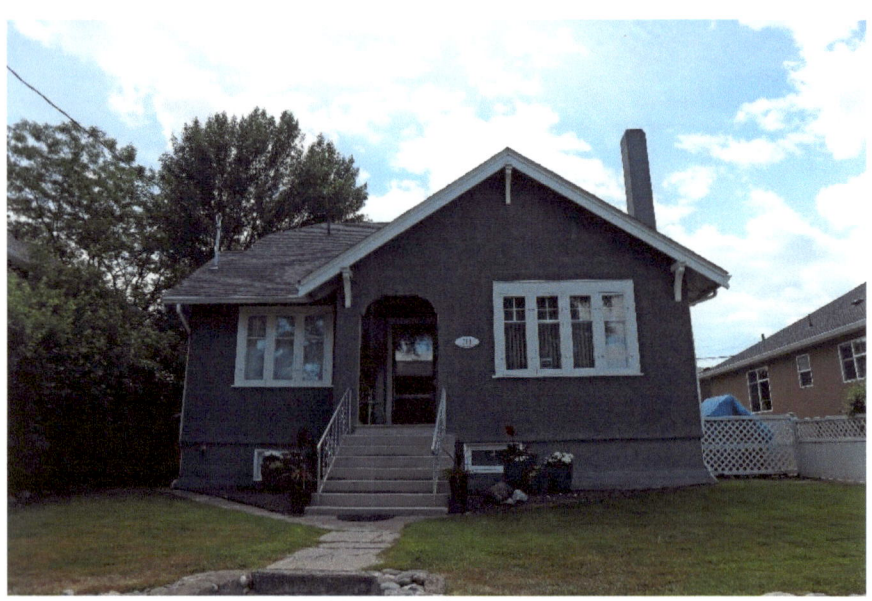
611 Nicola Street

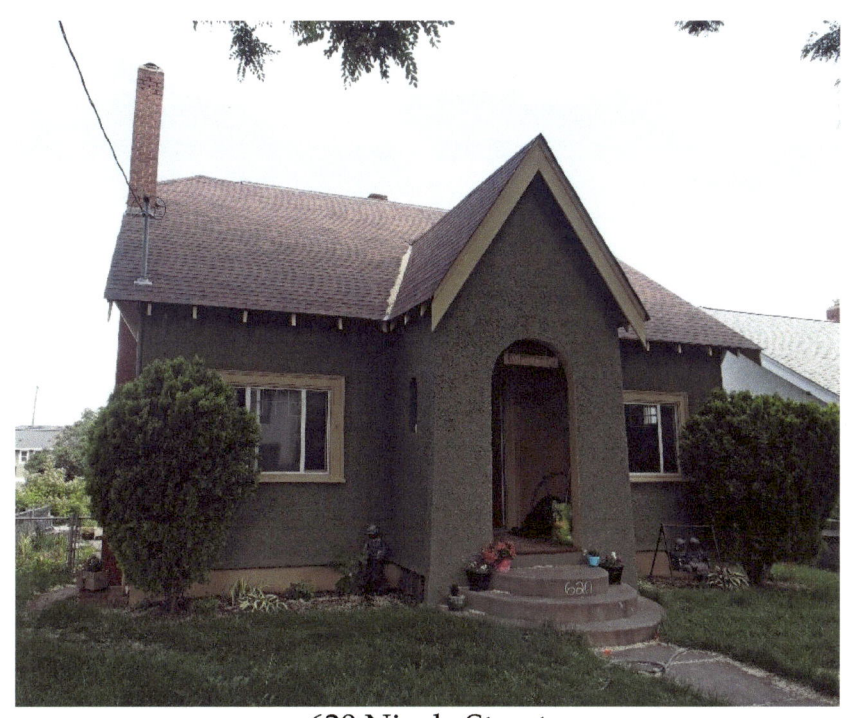

620 Nicola Street

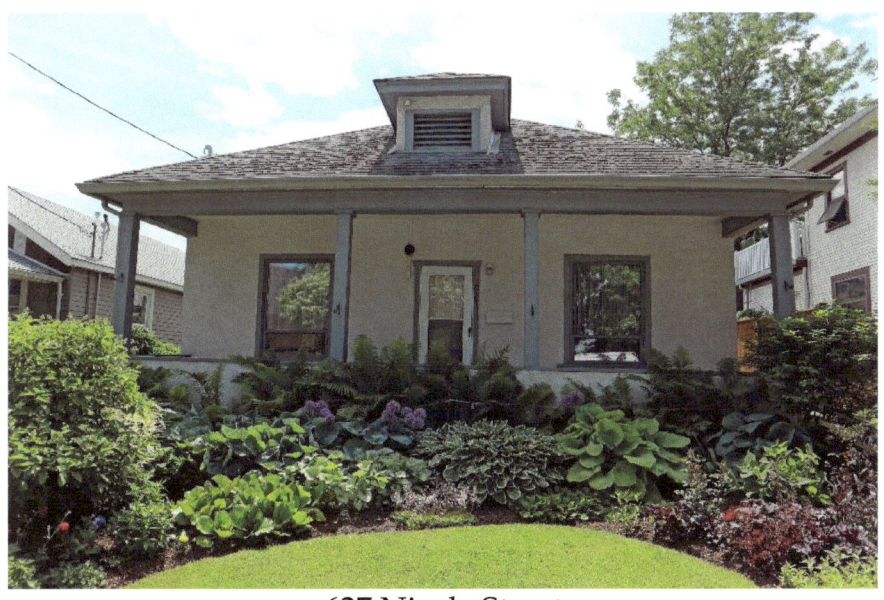

627 Nicola Street

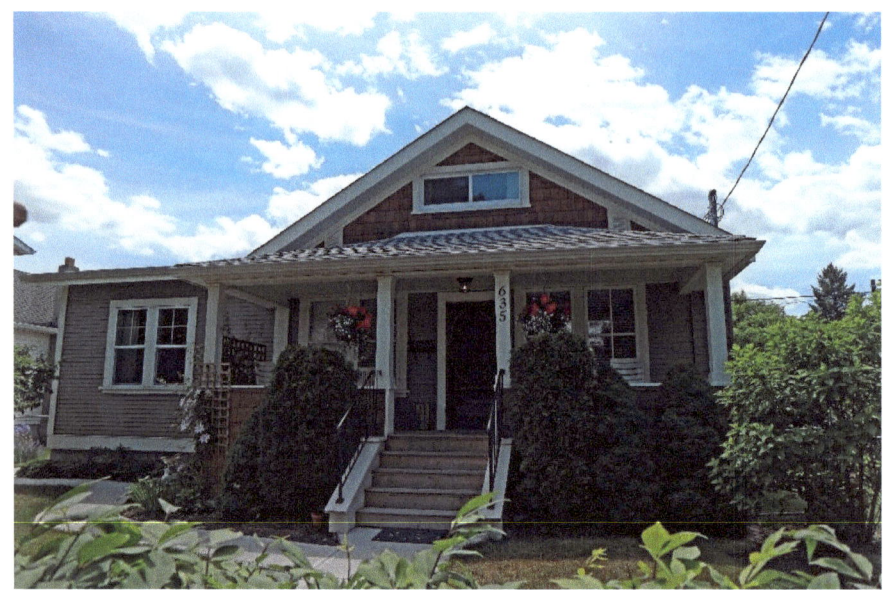
635 Nicola Street

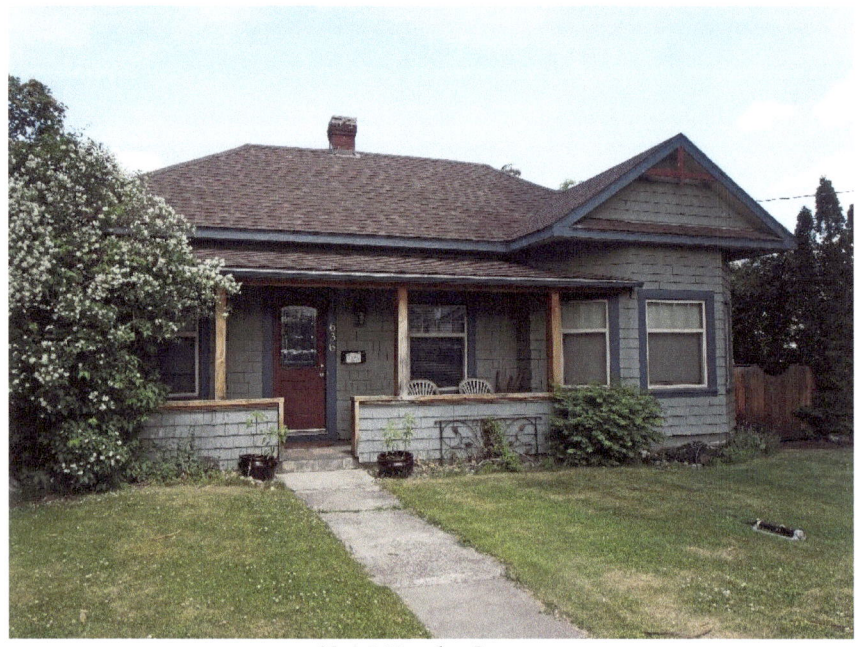
636 Nicola Street

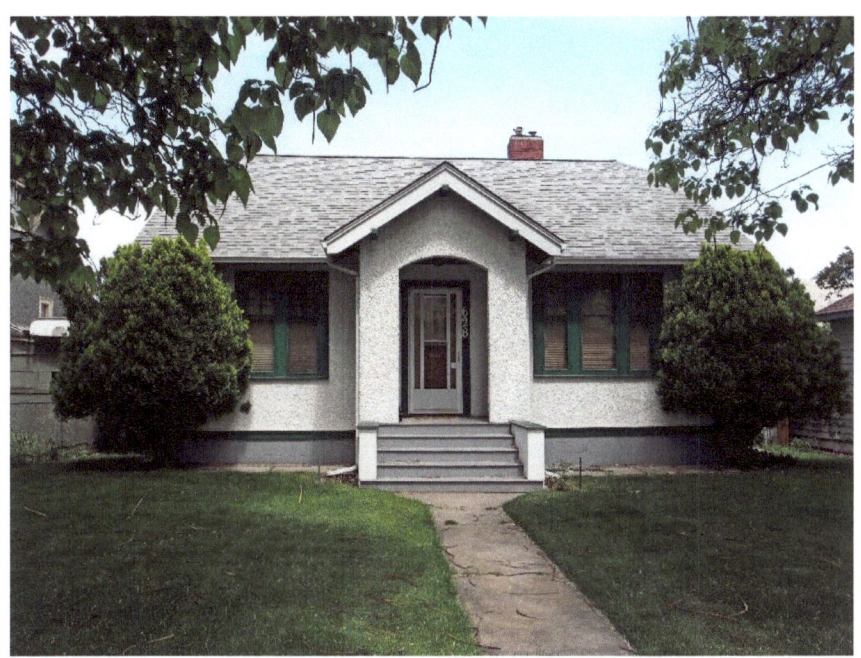

628 Nicola Street

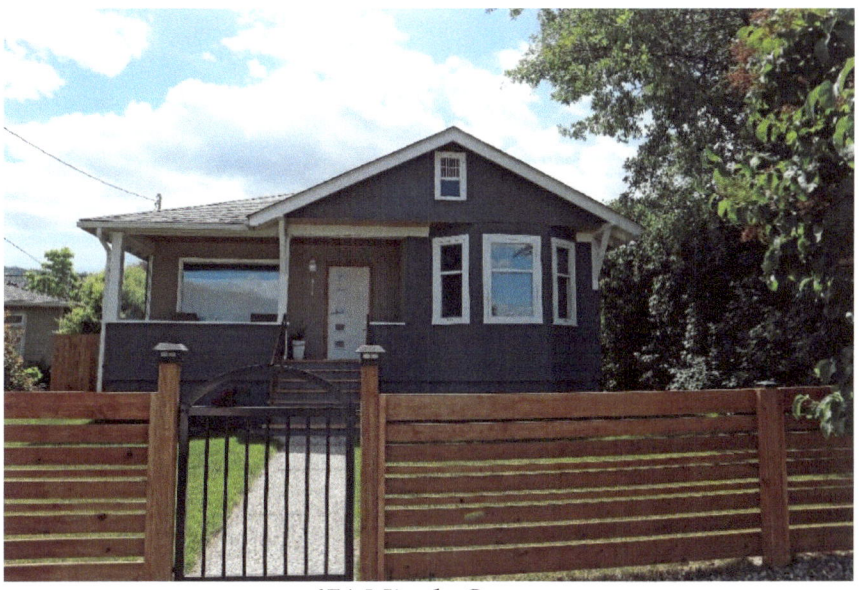

651 Nicola Street

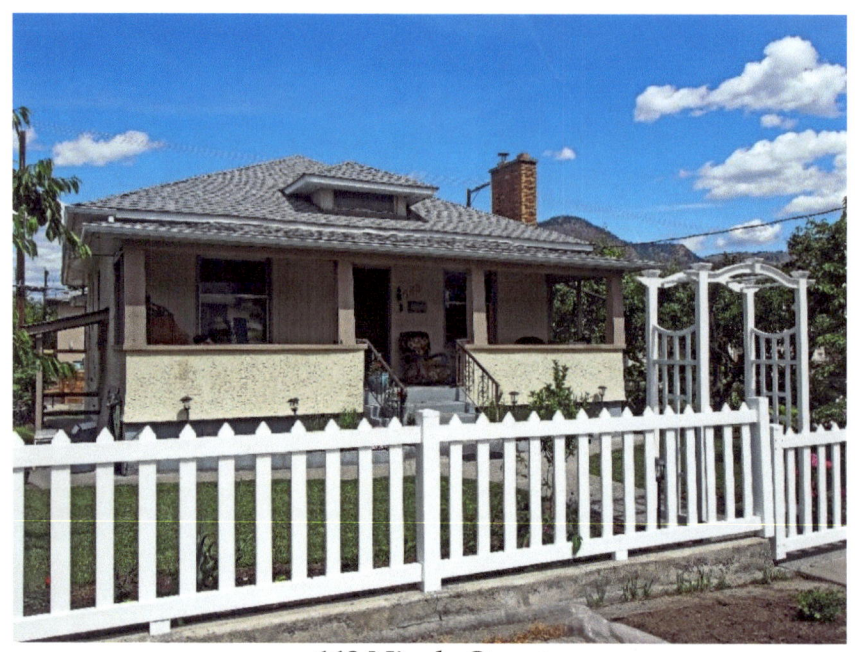

668 Nicola Street

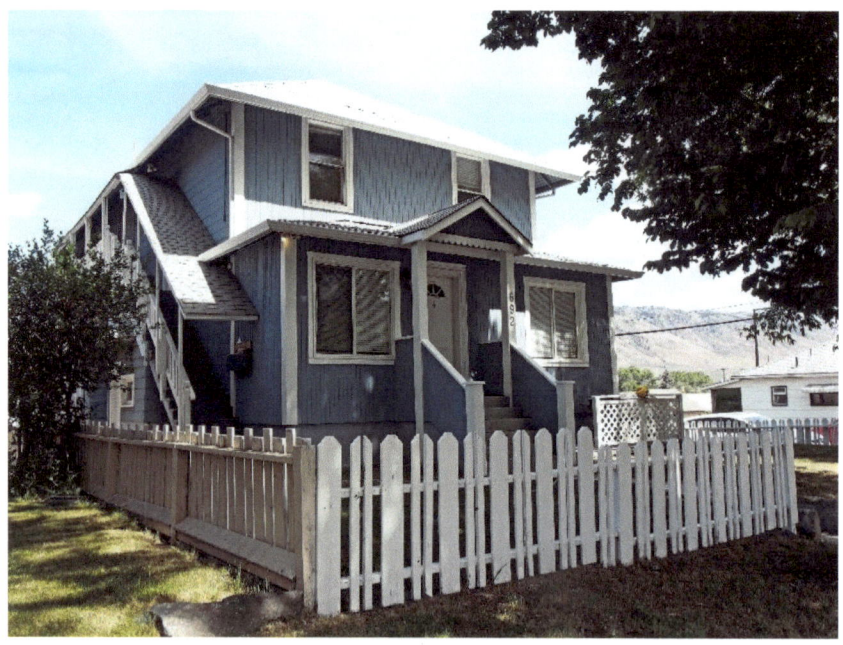

692 Nicola Street

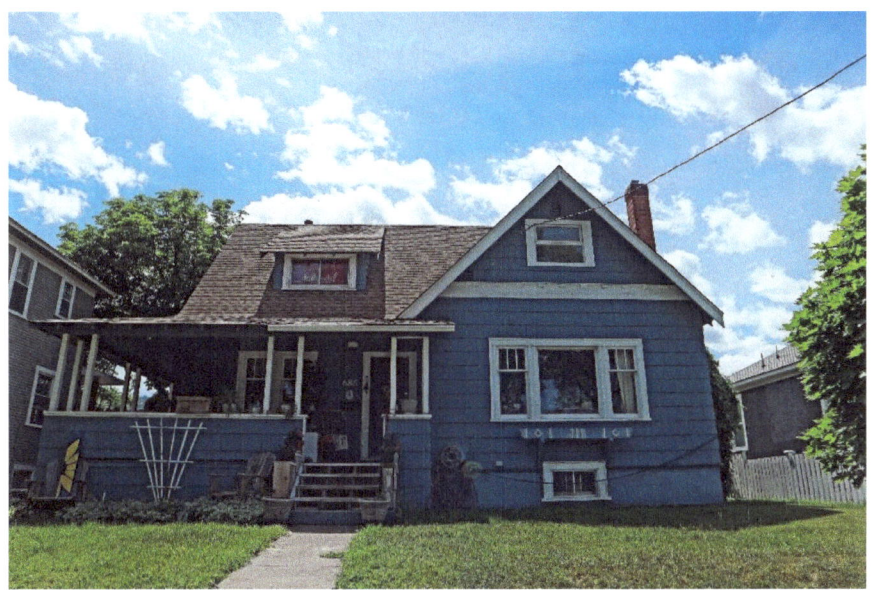

685 Nicola Street –William and Edna Helen Normand House - This attractive bungalow was built in 1936 by William and Edna Helen Normand, ranchers from Pritchard.

Inside, are beautiful wood floors inlaid with oak. The original door frames and doors are all in place including two sets of double French doors with leaded glass. Nine-foot ceilings, original fixtures and crystal door knobs are still to be found throughout the house as well as built-in cupboards in the hall.

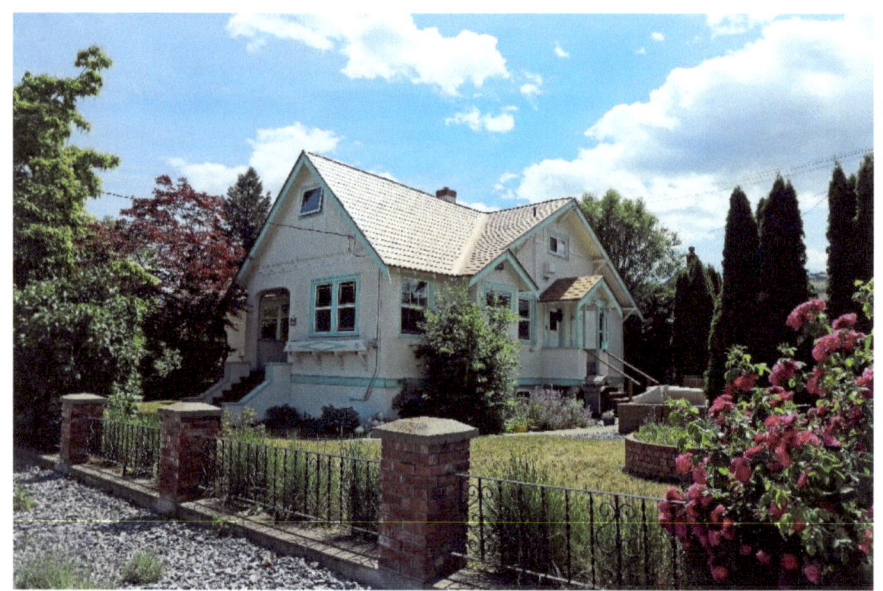

707 Nicola Street

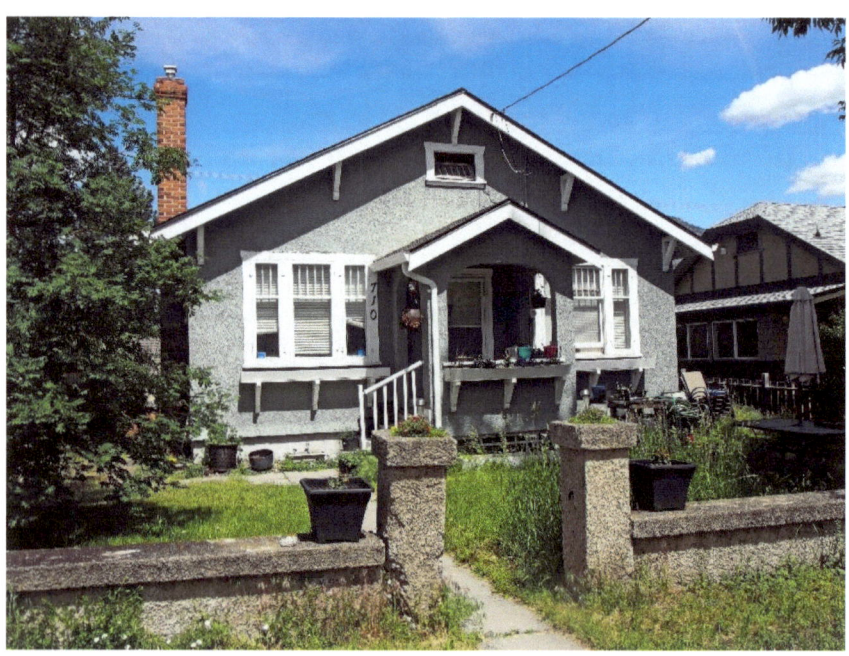

710 Nicola Street

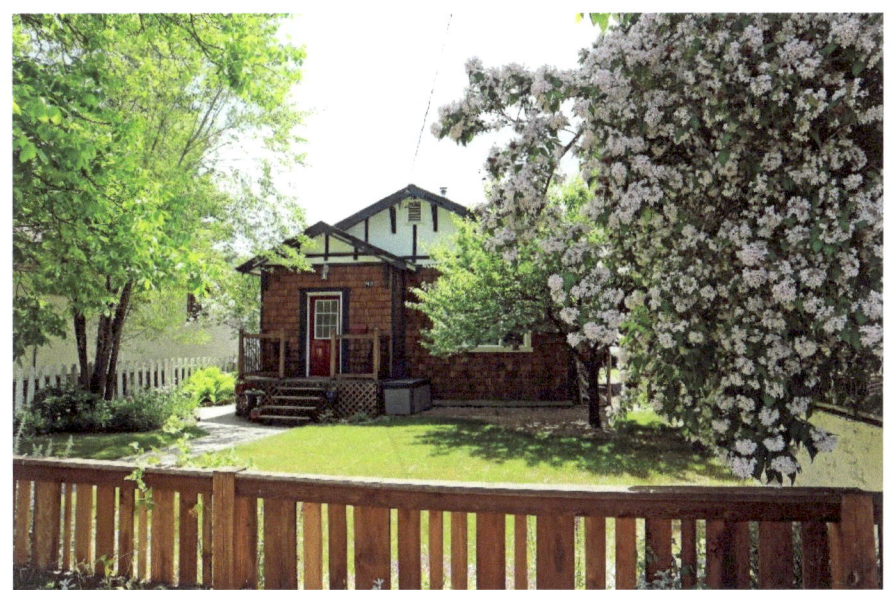

717 Nicola Street

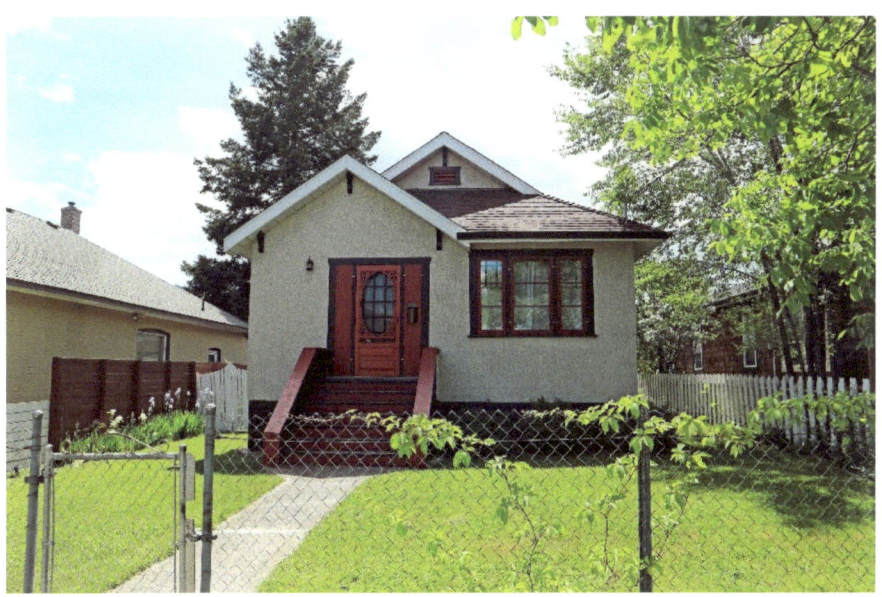

723 Nicola Street

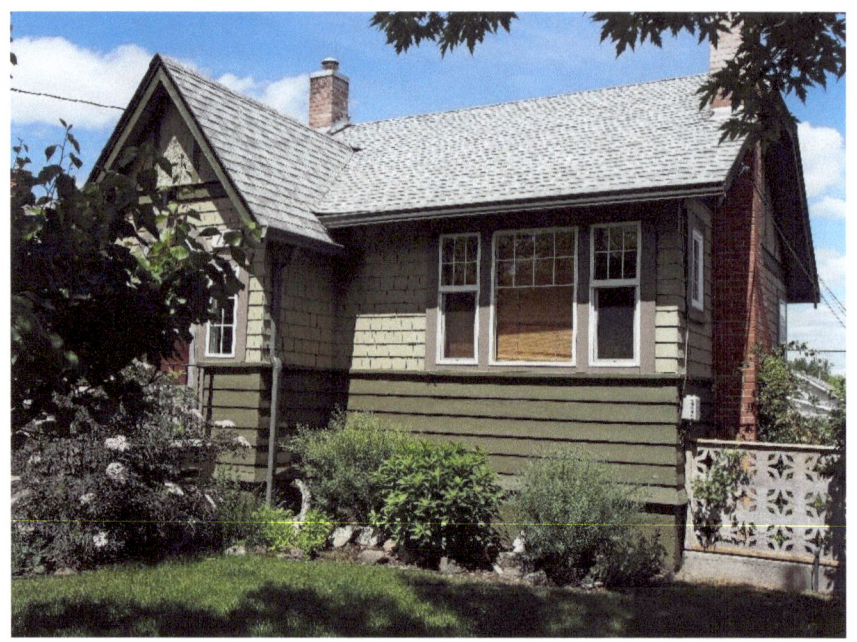

724 Nicola Street

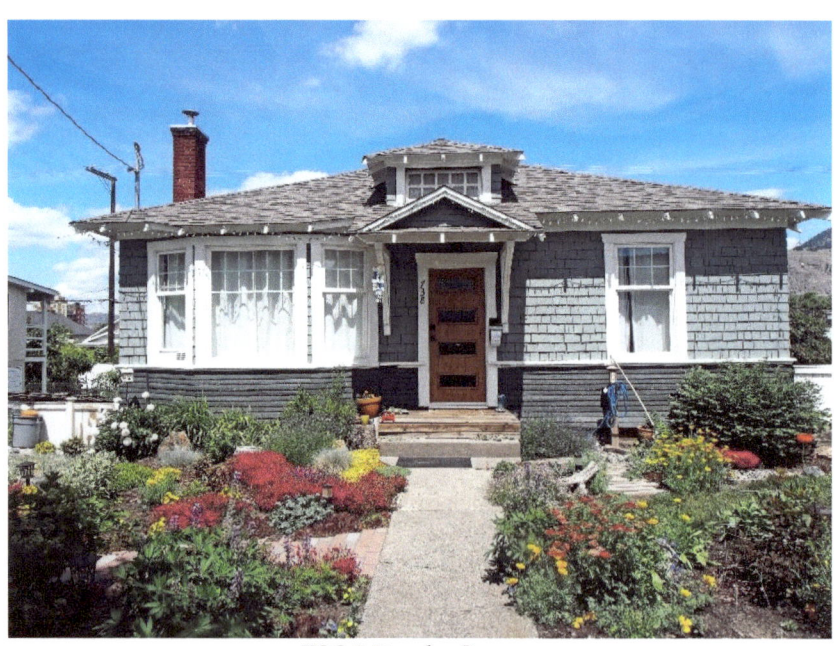

738 Nicola Street

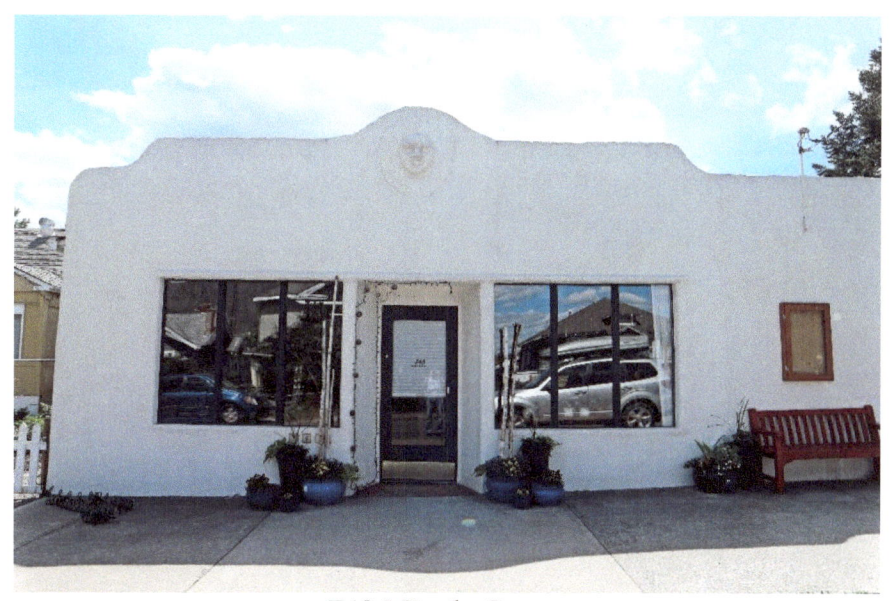

743 Nicola Street

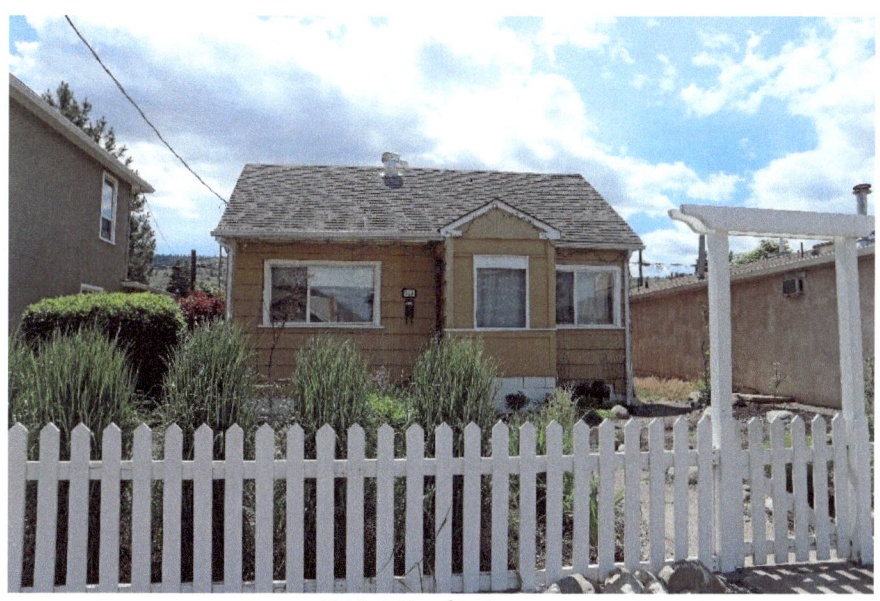

749 Nicola Street

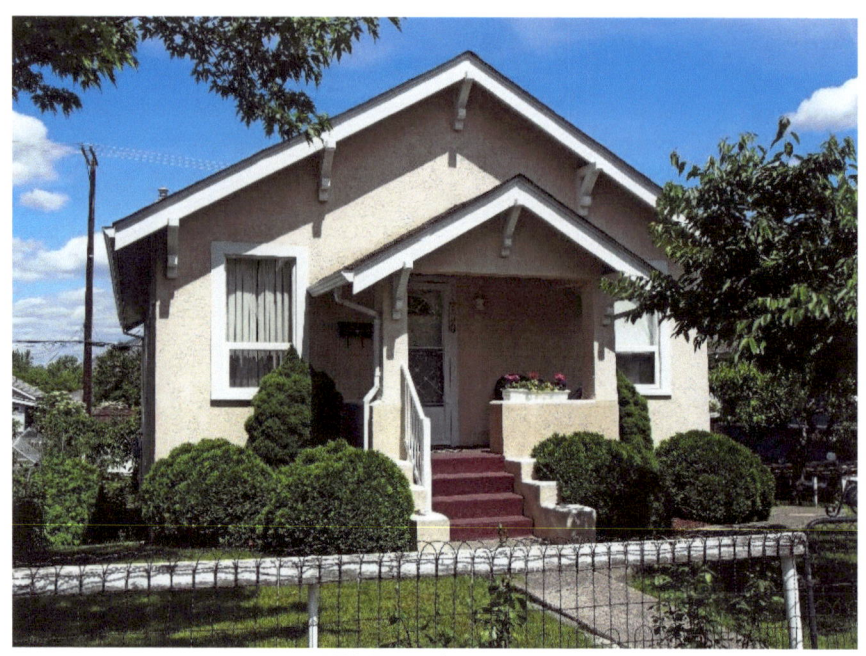

750 Nicola Street

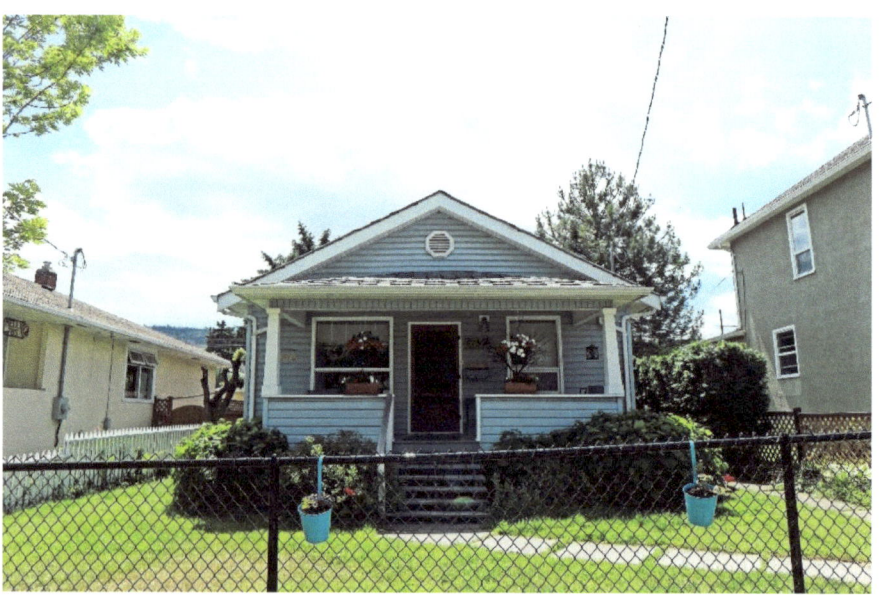

759 Nicola Street

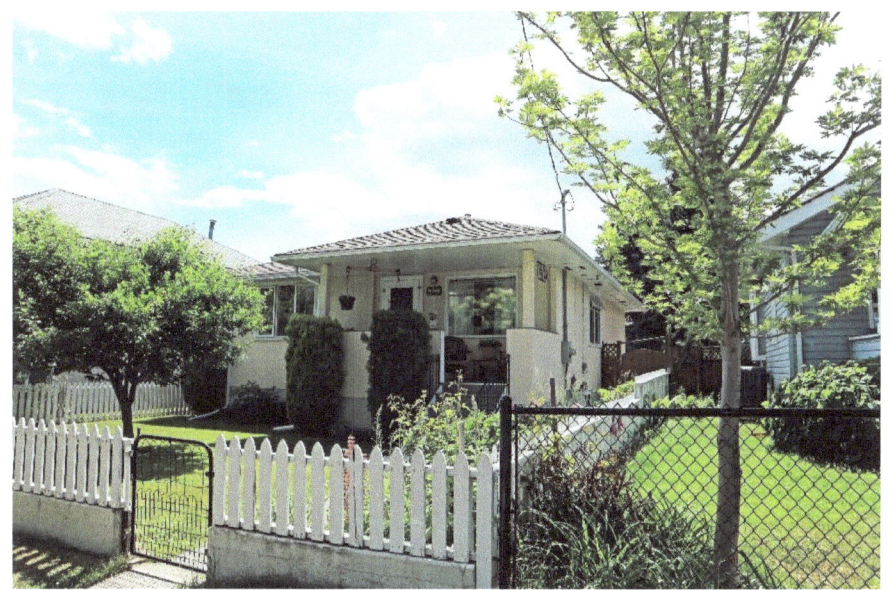

765 Nicola Street

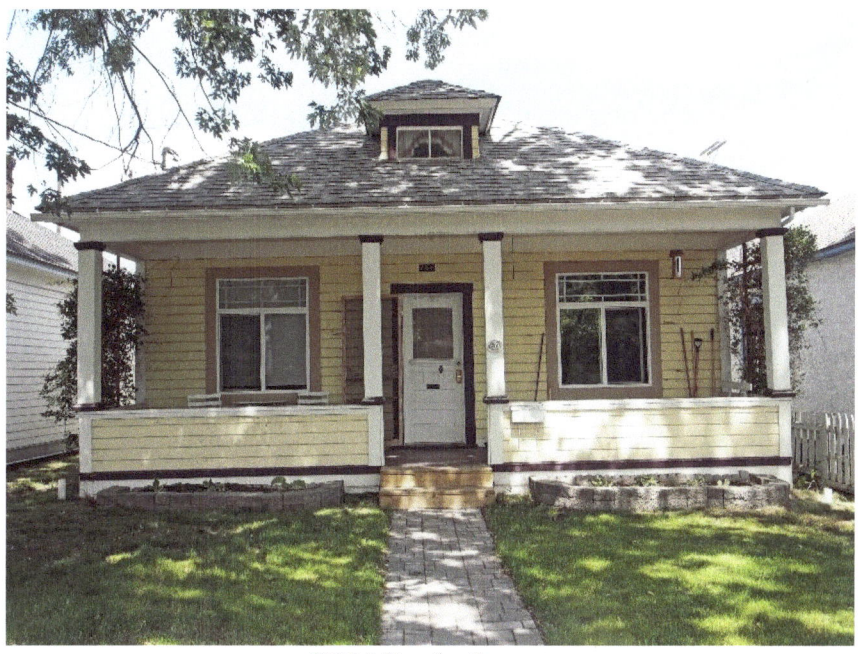

766 Nicola Street

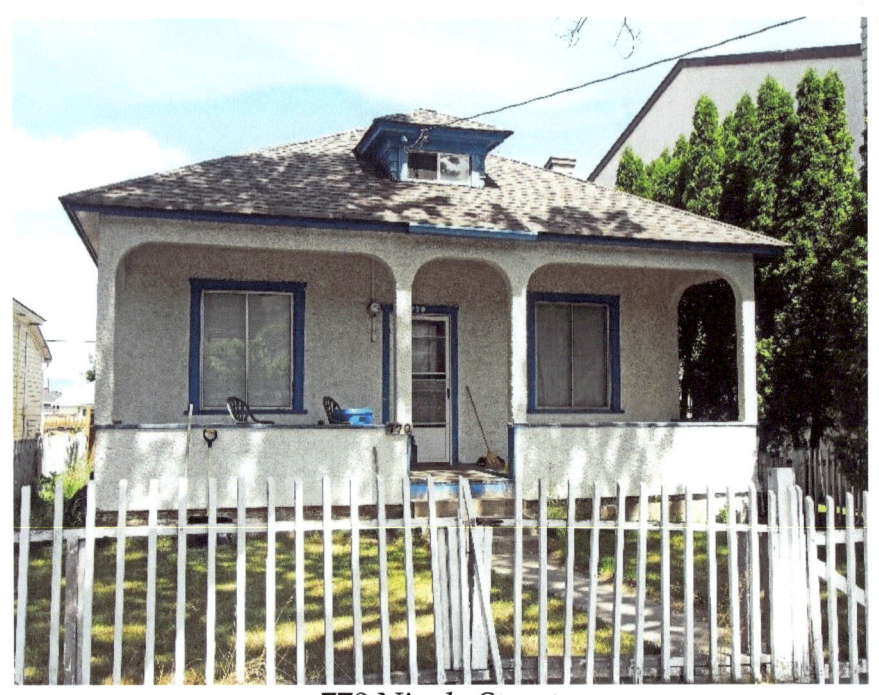

770 Nicola Street

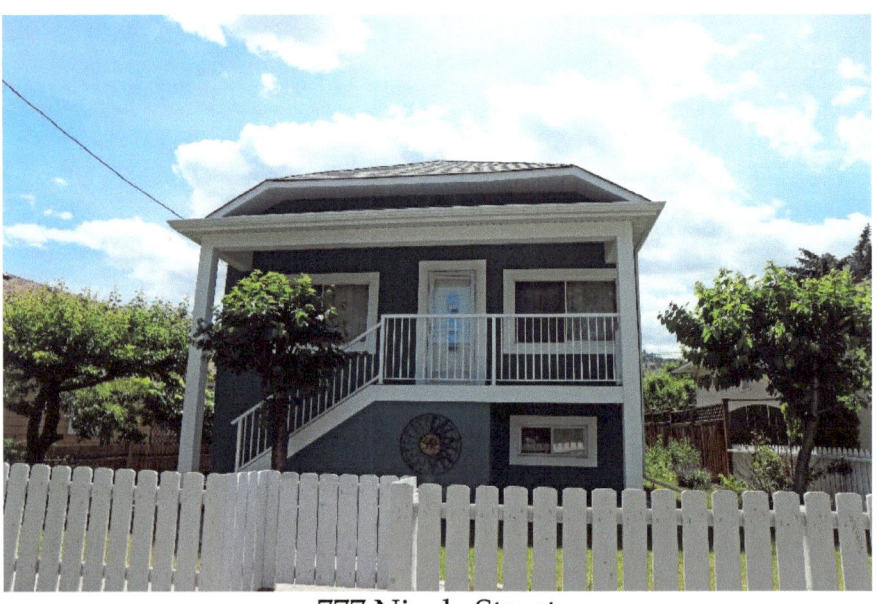

777 Nicola Street

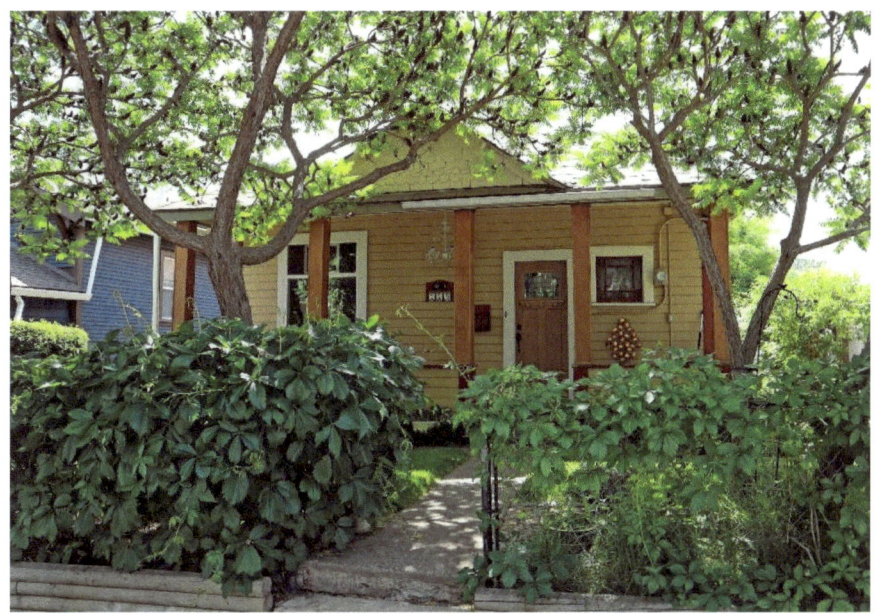

779 Nicola Street

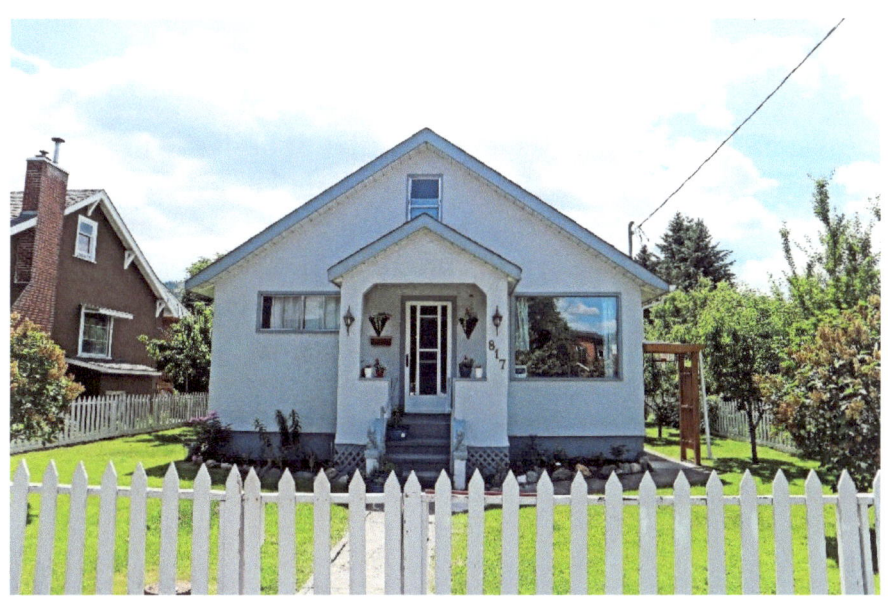

817 Nicola Street

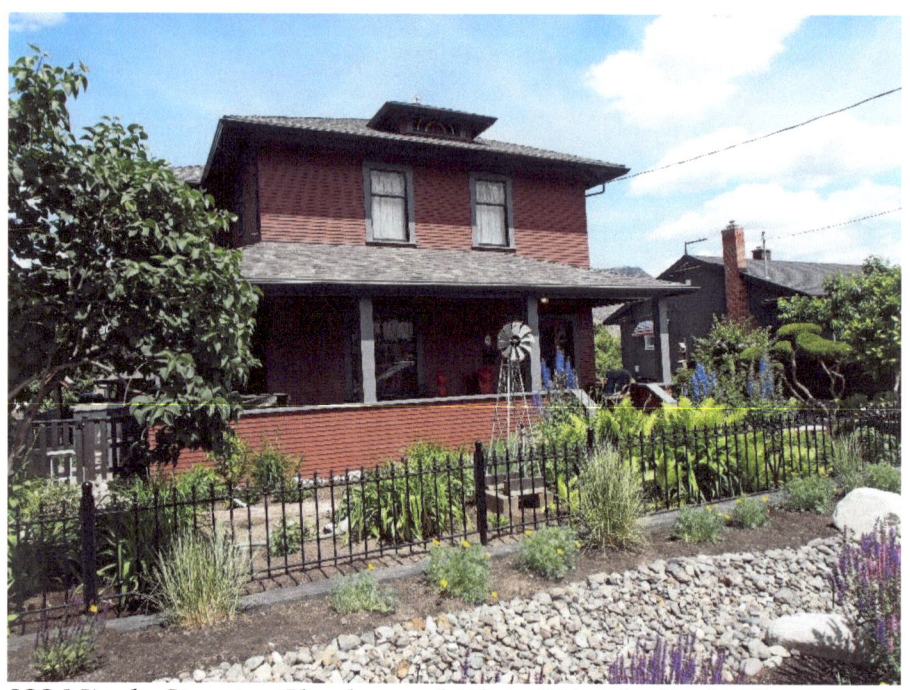

822 Nicola Street – Charles and Clara Hirst built the first house on this block in 1912 in the popular classic box style. The house was subsequently bought by Robert McCall in 1921 who was elected the Police Commissioner in 1926. The house has been extensively restored to its original condition with clapboard siding, v board soffits, wood rafter fascia, and leaded glass panel windows.

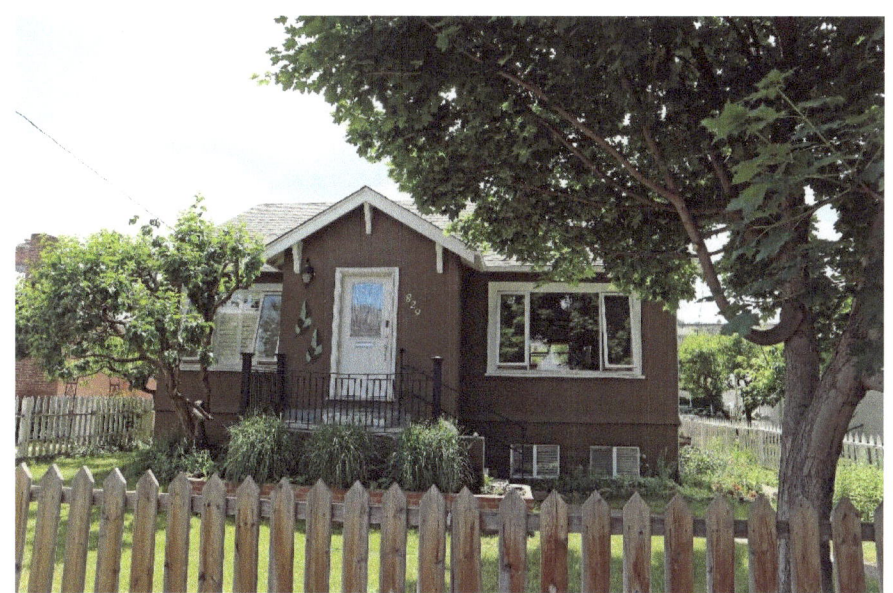

829 Nicola Street

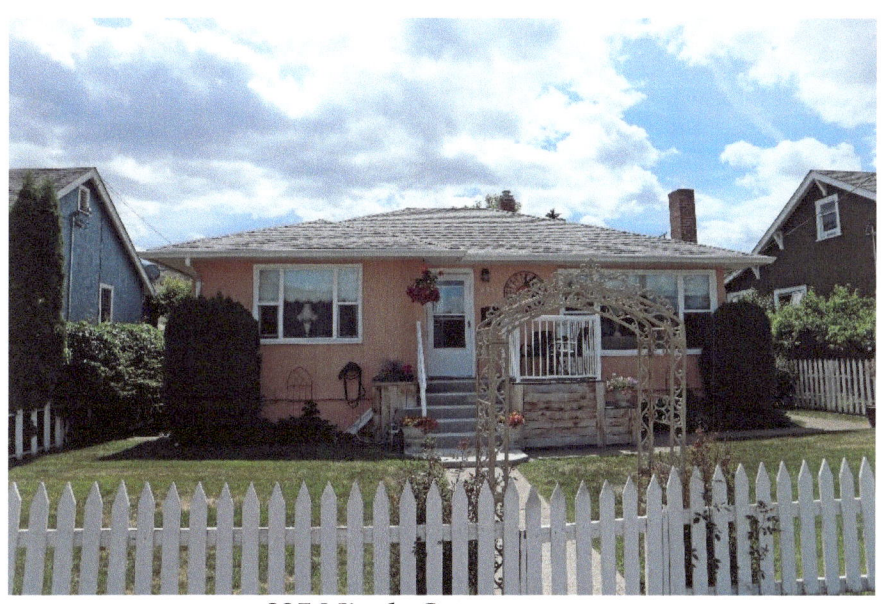

835 Nicola Street - stucco

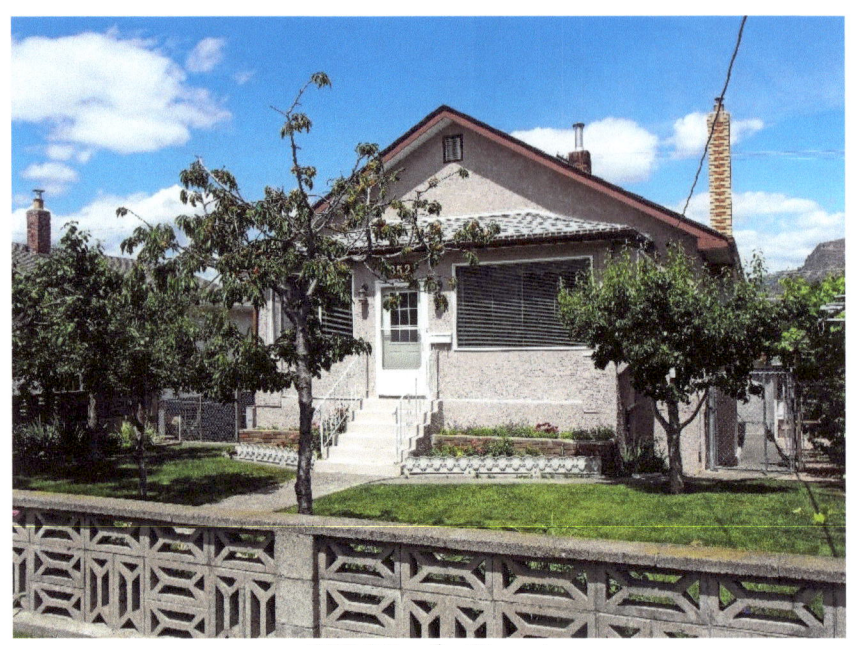
852 Nicola Street

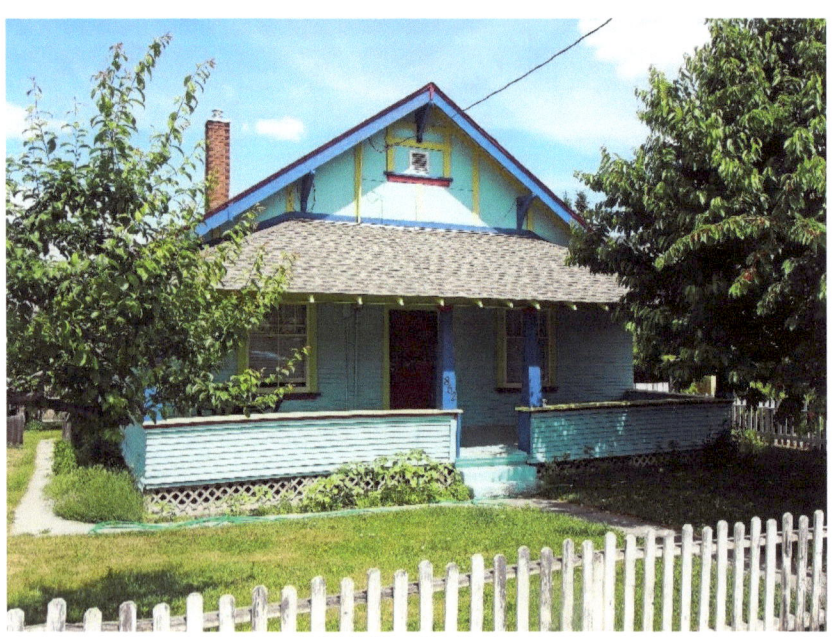
862 Nicola Street

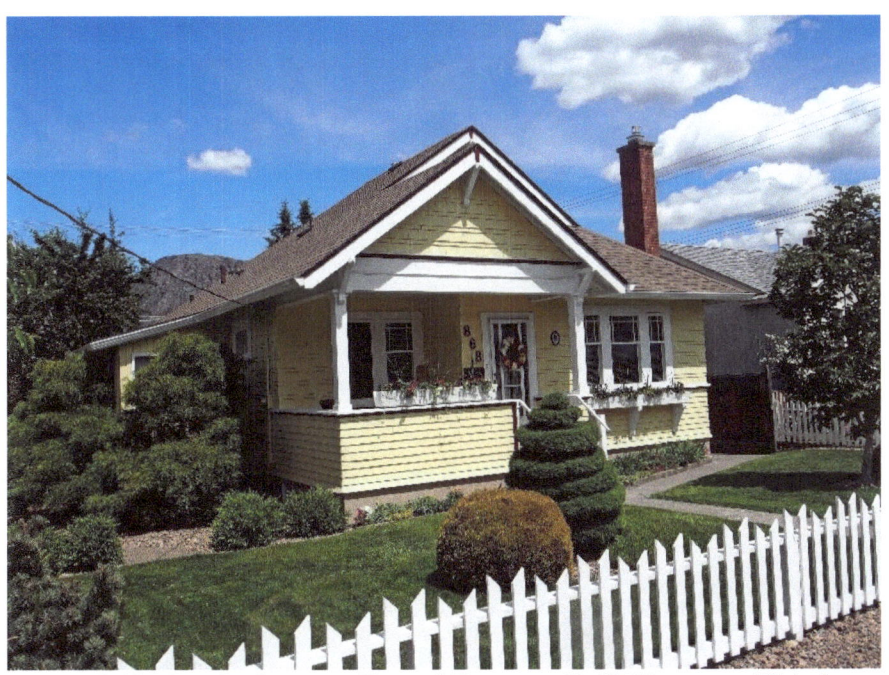

868 Nicola Street - Royal Dayton Bell House – This late Craftsman style house was built just before the outbreak of World War II by R.D. Bell. Bell was a contractor and carpenter, and given the quality of this house, he probably built it himself.

The outside of the house is sided in double rows of cedar shingles. The verandah is getting smaller, as was typical of this period, but it is still a comfortable size by today's standards and features a wide top railing and slender columns with decorative moldings. Pretty window boxes complete the cottage-like quality of the house.

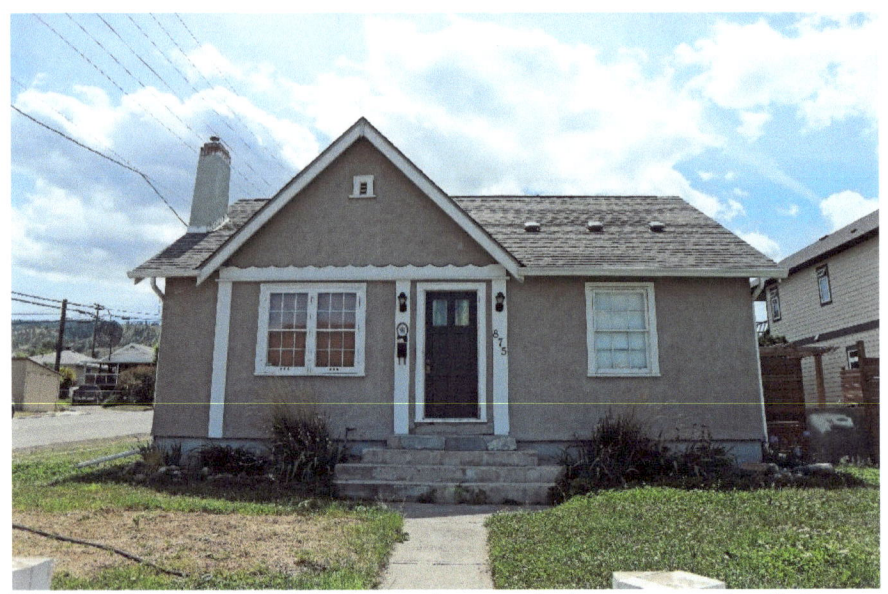

875 Nicola Street – This Bungalow style house was built in 1944. The exterior has original plaster stucco siding, wood soffits and fascia, multi-pane wood frame windows and a scallop frame to accent the front side.

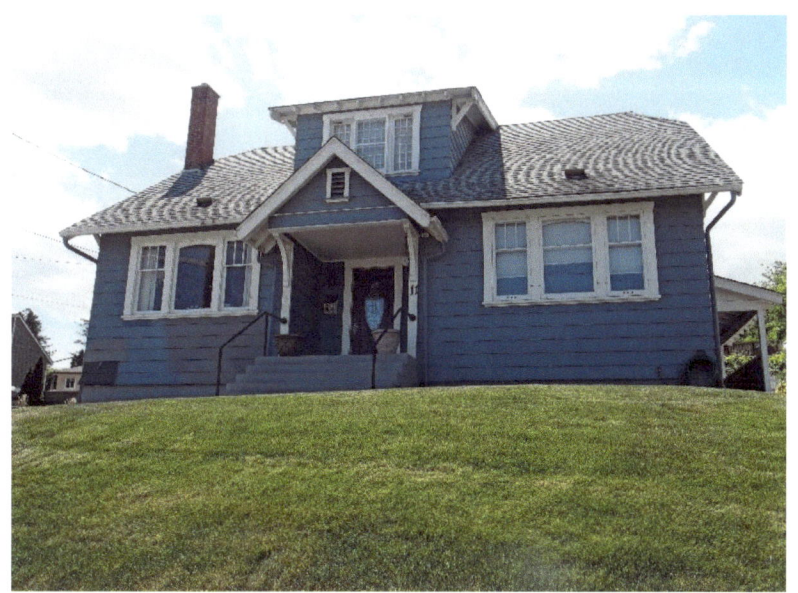

11 Nicola Street West

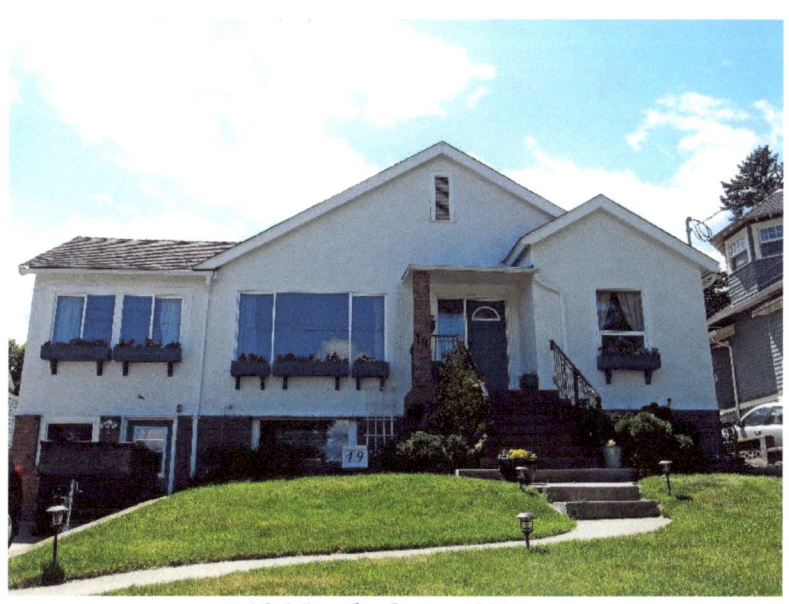

19 Nicola Street West

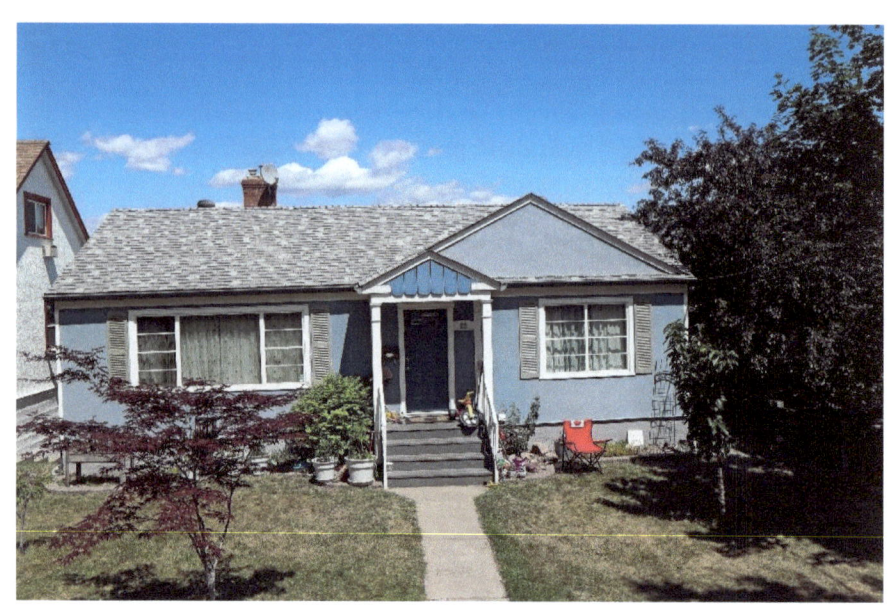

22 Nicola Street West

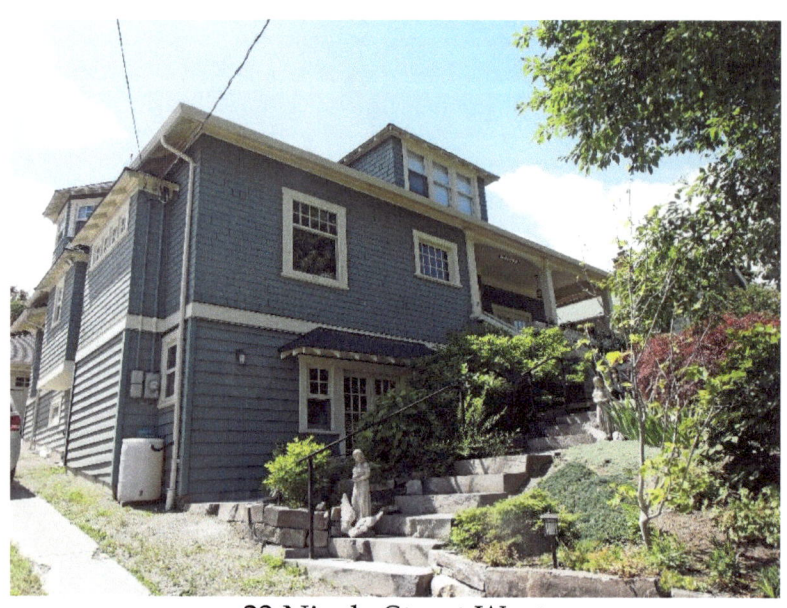

23 Nicola Street West

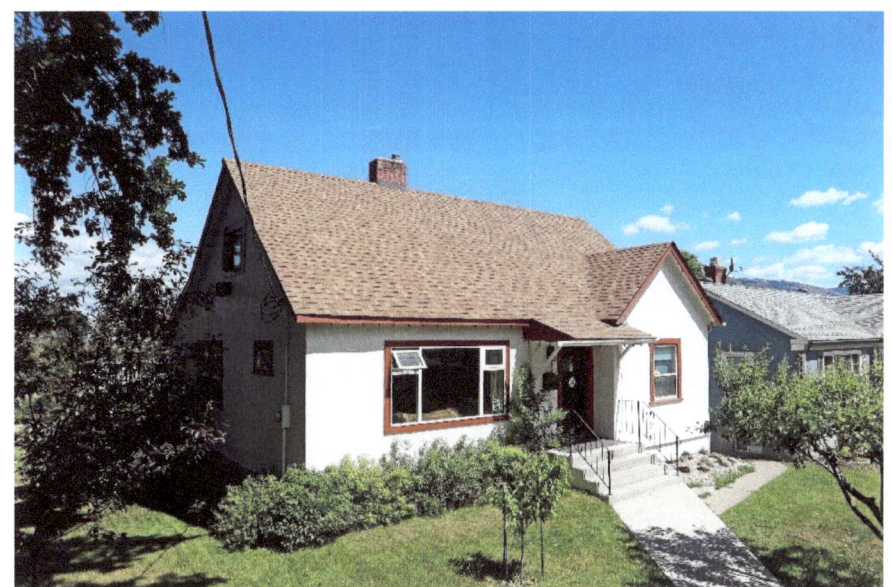

28 Nicola Street West

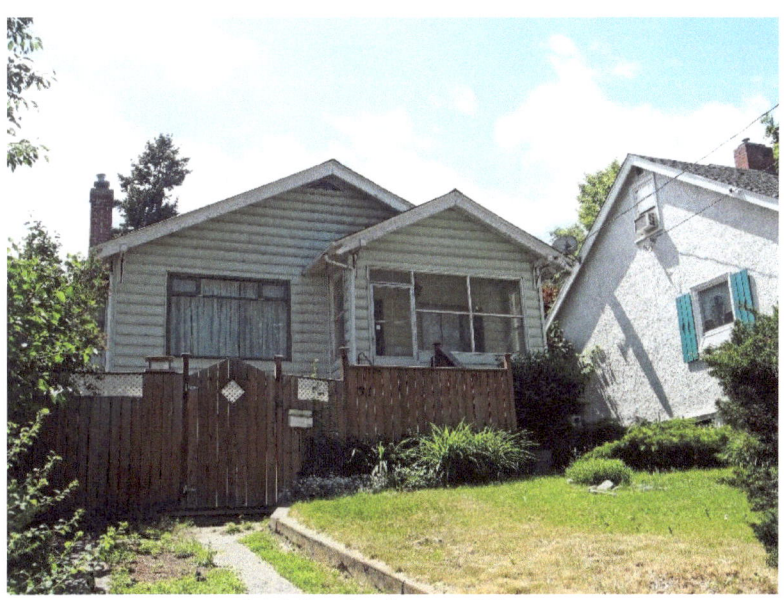

31 Nicola Street West

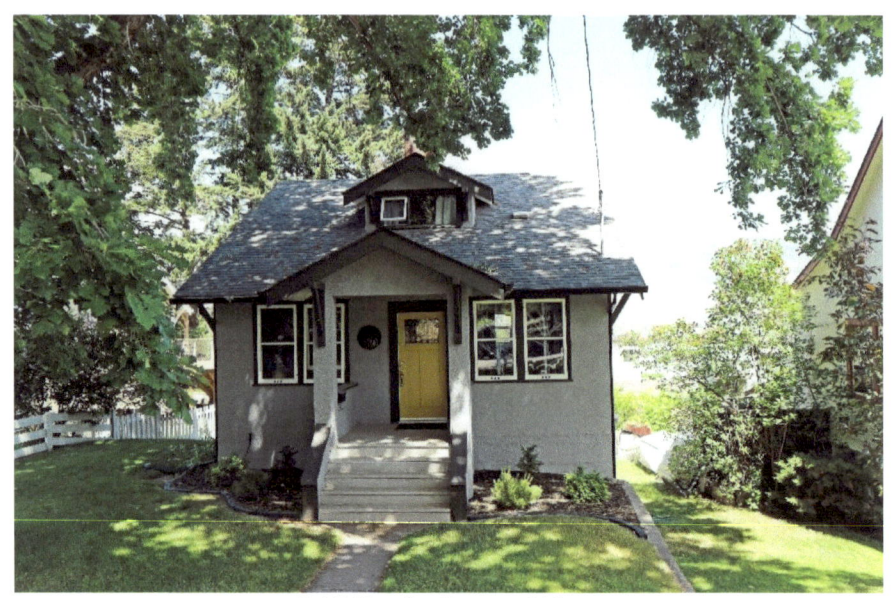

36 Nicola Street West

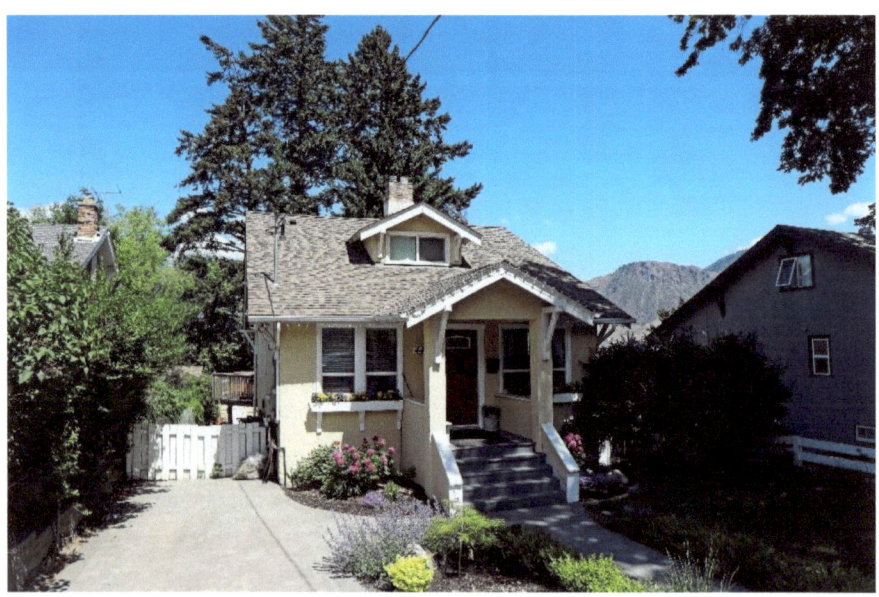

44 Nicola Street West

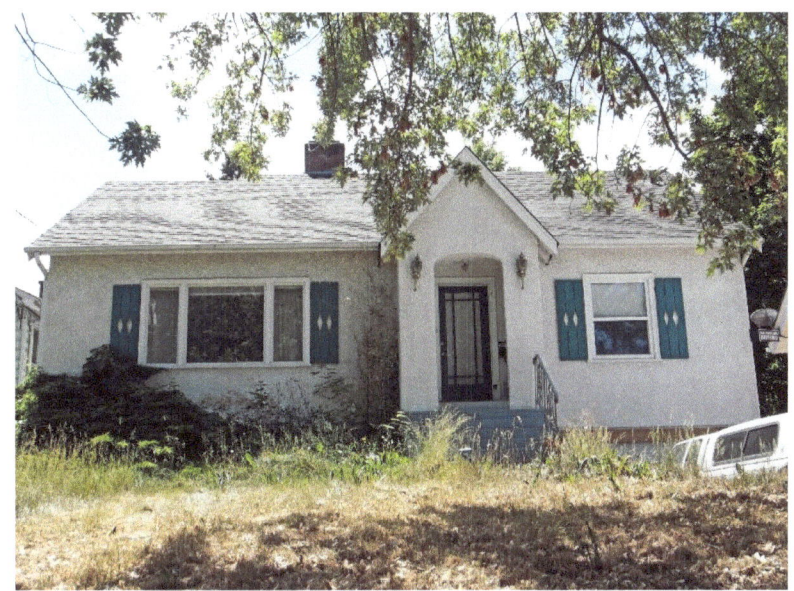

Nicola Street West

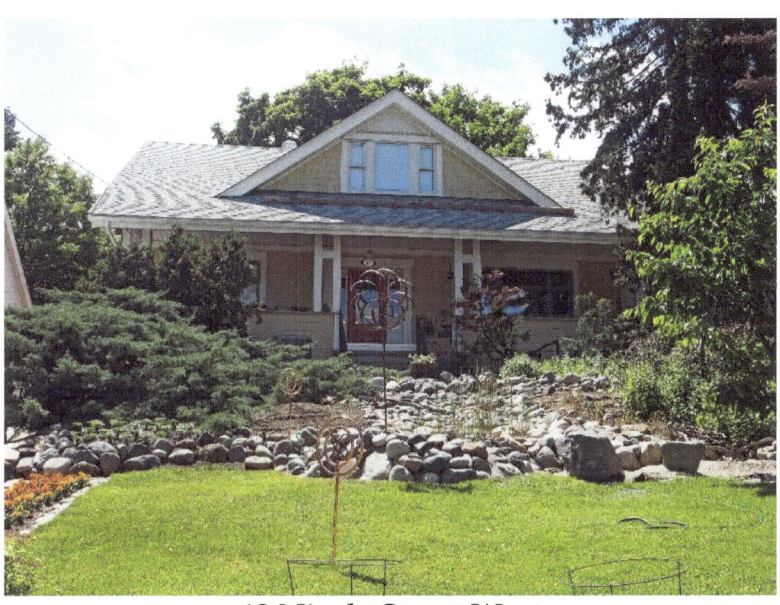

49 Nicola Street West

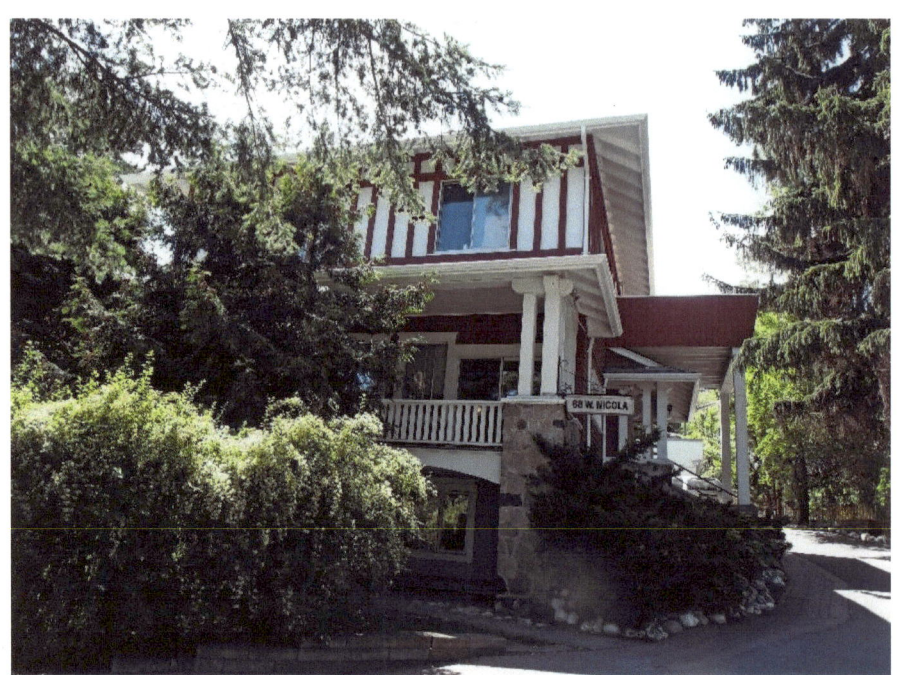

63 Nicola Street West – Frederick J. Fulton House - When this mansion was built in 1912, it sat almost alone on top of the hill. The property connected to the house covered a hectare of land on both sides of the house and up the slope behind it to Columbia Street. Frederick Fulton came to Kamloops in 1889 as one of the first lawyers in town. The firm he helped to found is still operating in Kamloops today and is the second oldest law firm in B.C.

The exterior of this grand house remains much the same as it was when first built, however, a balcony and staircase have been added over the front door. The paint colors and exterior siding are authentic, but the roof has been shingled with asphalt shingles instead of cedar shingles for fire safety reasons. The house is a Tudor style with attractive stone work and an impressive facade.

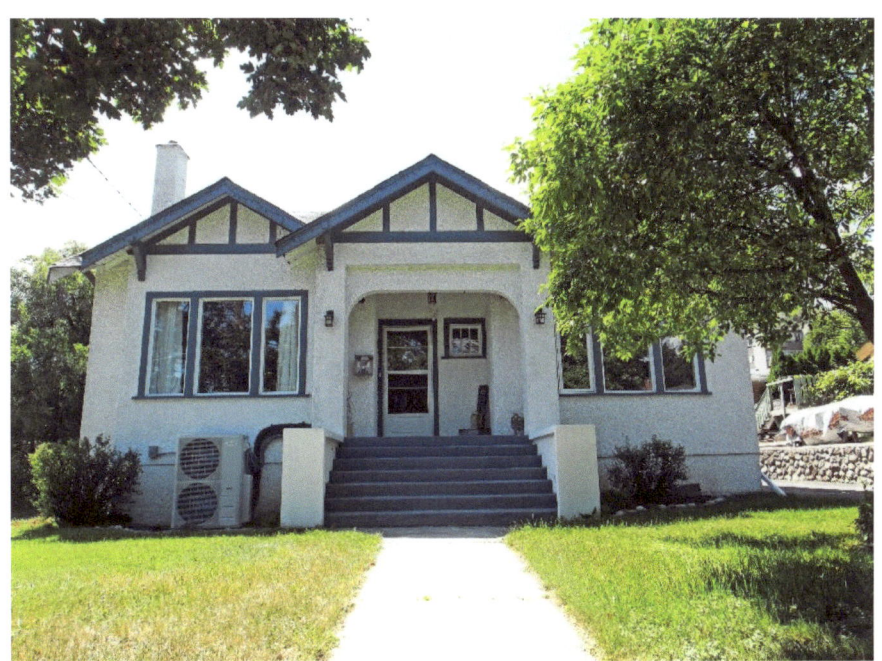

Nicola Street West

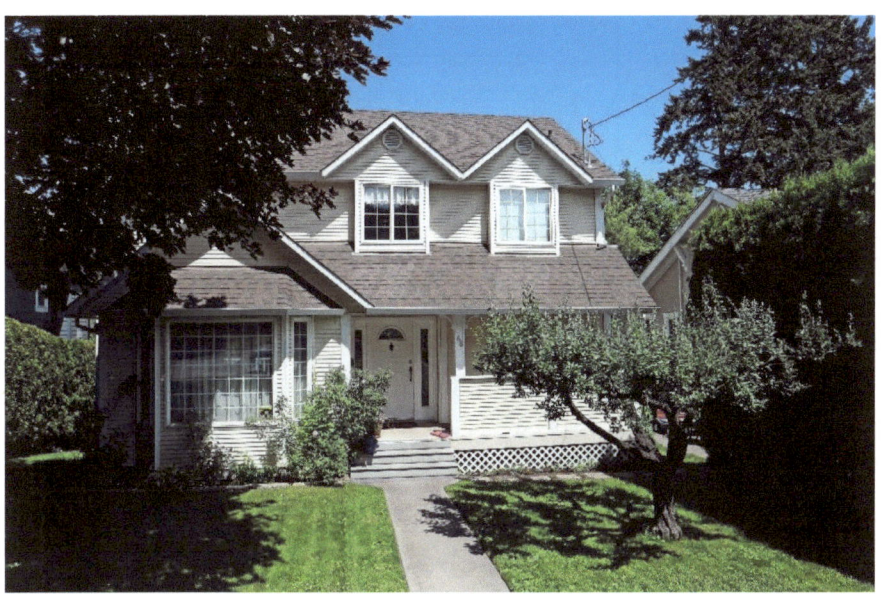

68 Nicola Street West

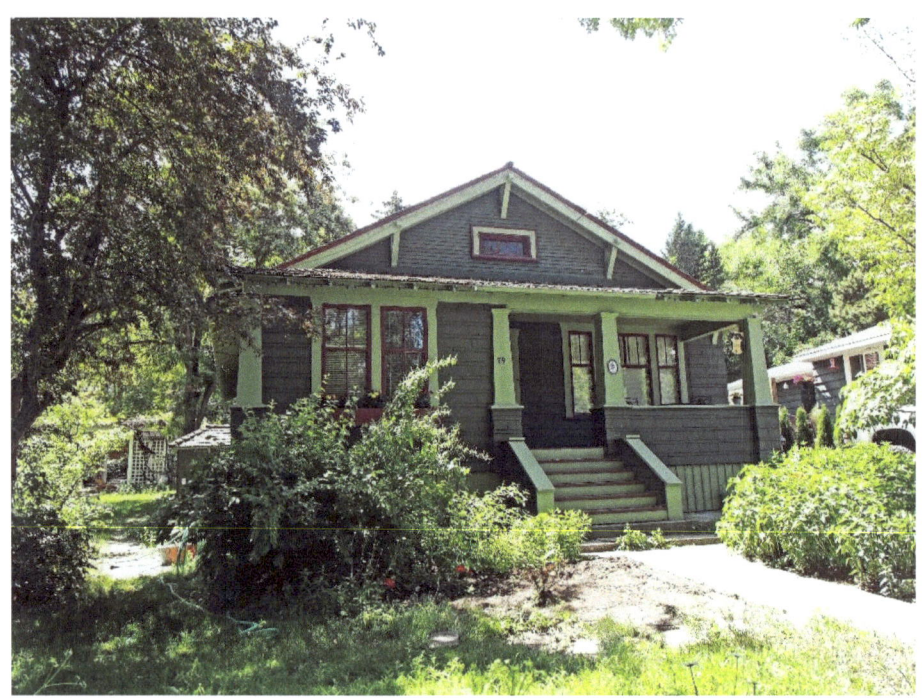

79 Nicola Street West –Joseph Stoodley House – Joseph Octavius Stoodley served Secretary-Treasurer of the Kamloops School Board, School Trustee, Truant Officer and City Collector at City Hall.

Built in 1926, the Stoodley Residence is a one-story Arts and Crafts bungalow. Typical of houses built in the 1920s, the house reflects the modern ideals of economy and domestic comfort. The typical features of the style are cedar shingle siding and roof, tapered veranda columns, multi-paned windows, wide window and door frames with simple moldings, exposed rafter ends, barge boards with triangular eave brackets, two small windows on either side of the chimney, and wide front and back verandas. There is a triangular window in the front gable. It has built-in flower boxes.

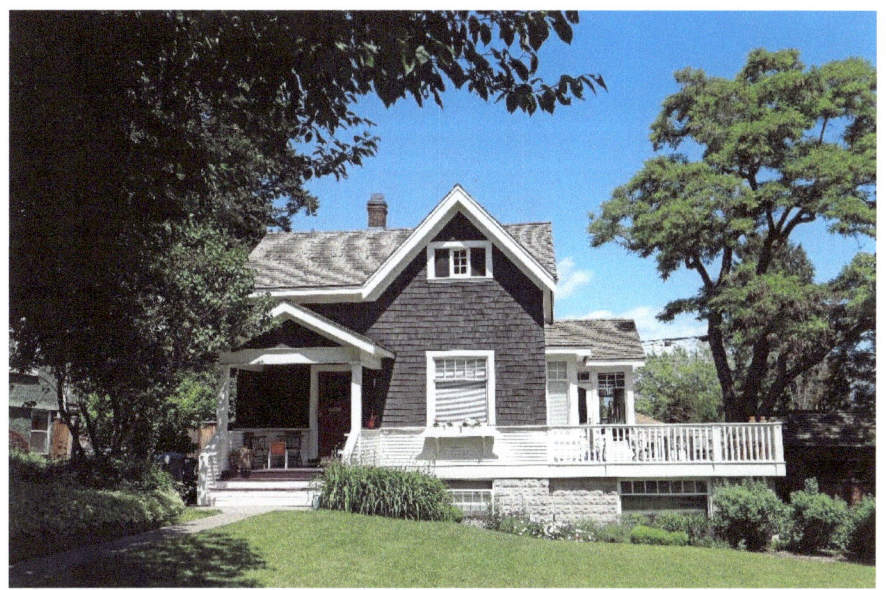

76 Nicola Street West

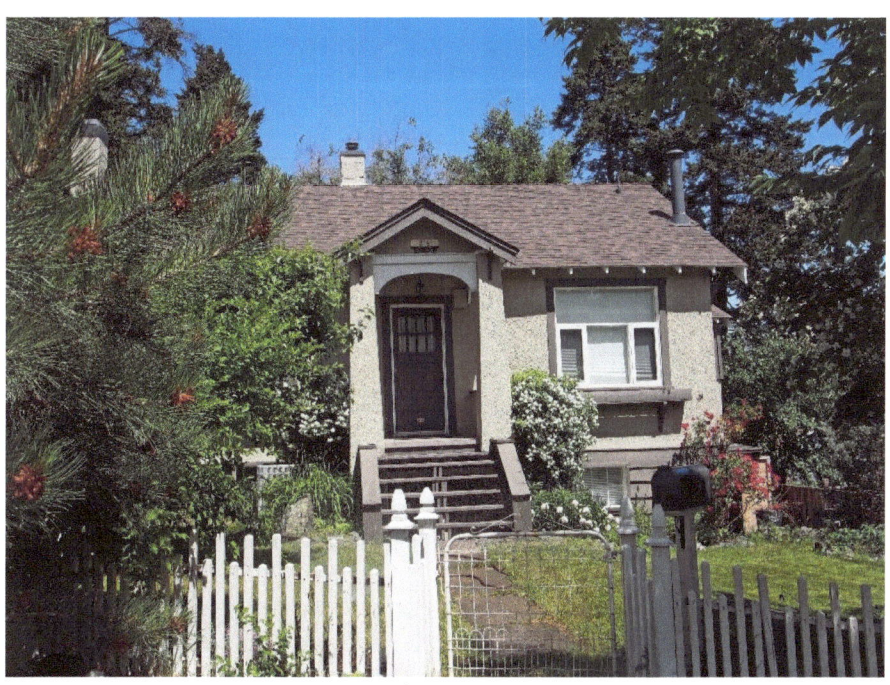

84 Nicola Street West

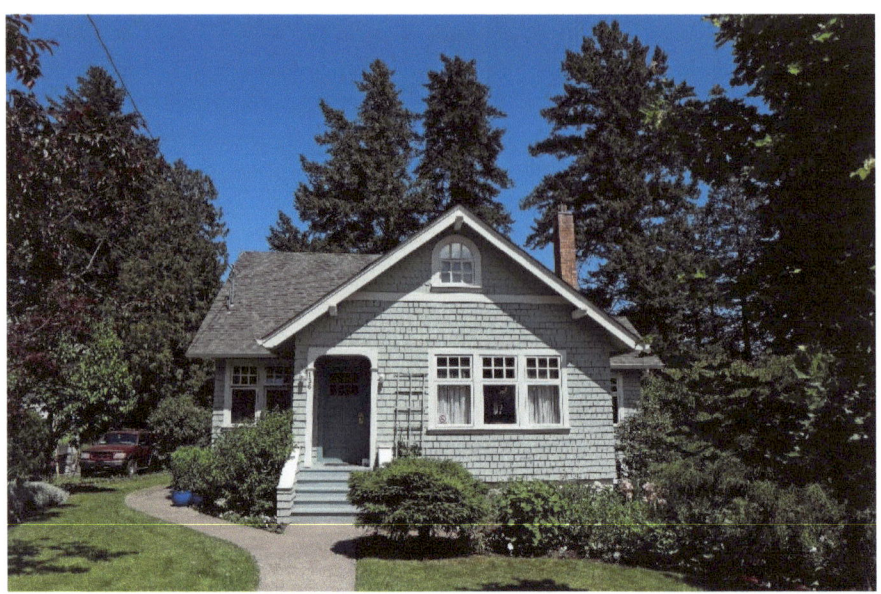

136 Nicola Street West –Rita Maude Best House - This house was built on the cusp of change in architectural styles. It has many traditional features reminiscent of the Arts & Crafts style including cedar shingle siding and roof, exposed rafter ends, wide barge boards, and multi-paned windows. However, the small front porch is a sign that this is a 1930s house. The front door is also distinctively 1930s in design.

This house is sitting on property which originally belonged to the big white house behind it, at 133 Battle Street West. The Pearse family began selling off lots beginning in the late 1920s and into the 1930s, so this house is one of the earliest. It belonged to Rita Best (nee MacLean) and her husband Lorne Sheridan Best. He was a machinist with the Canadian National Railway.

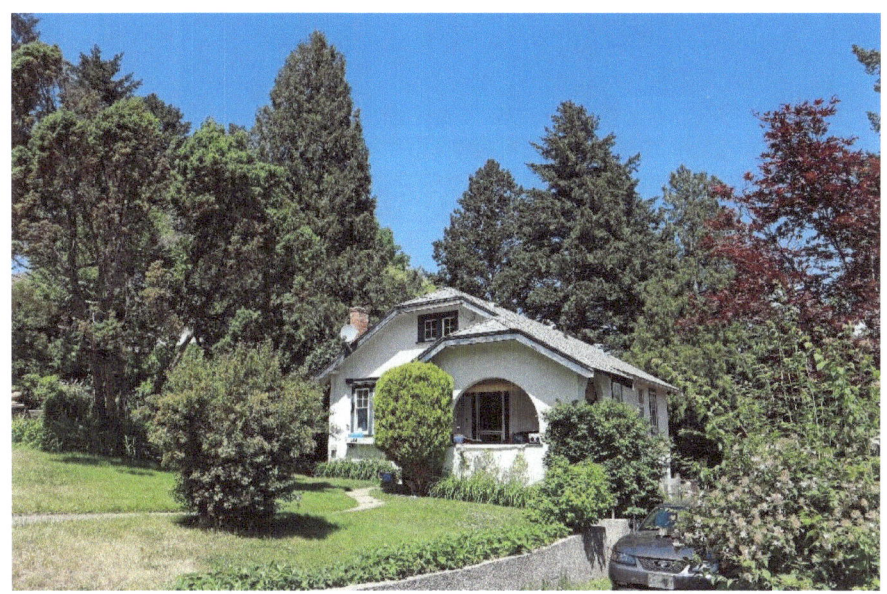

144 Nicola Street West – chipped gables

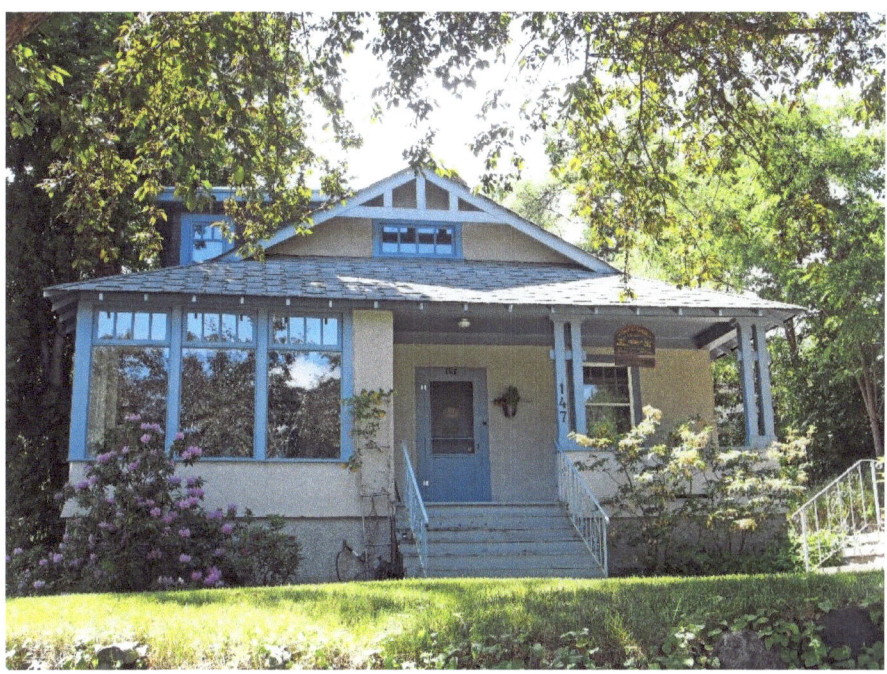

147 Nicola Street West

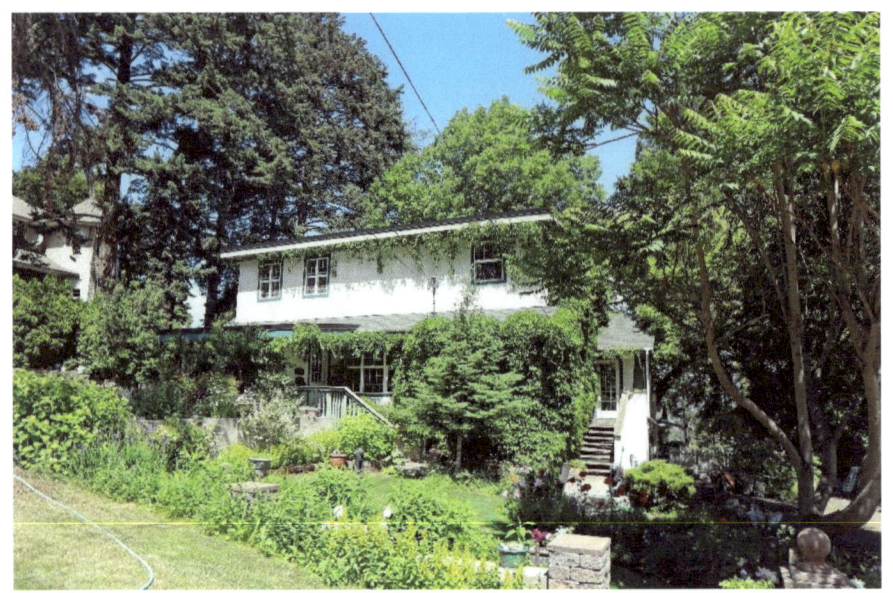
156 Nicola Street West

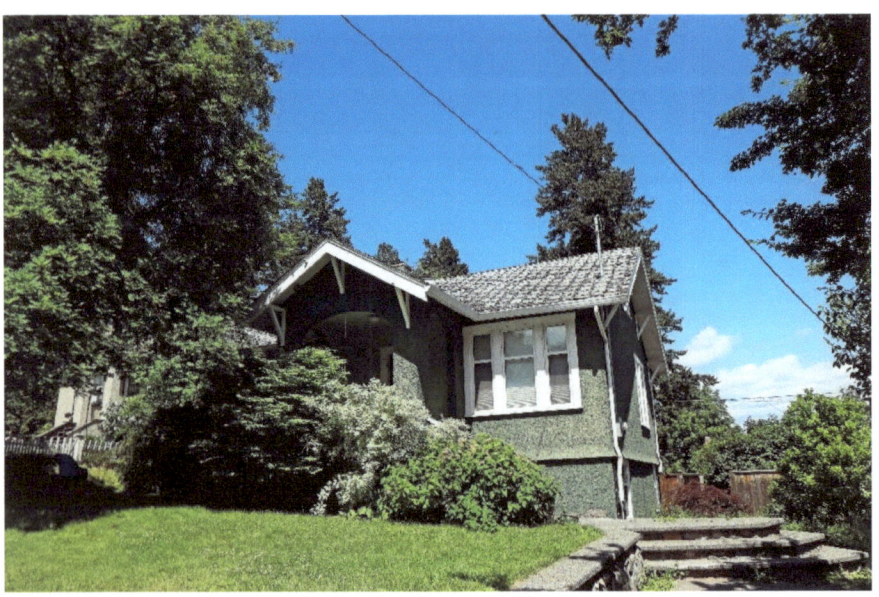
Nicola Street West

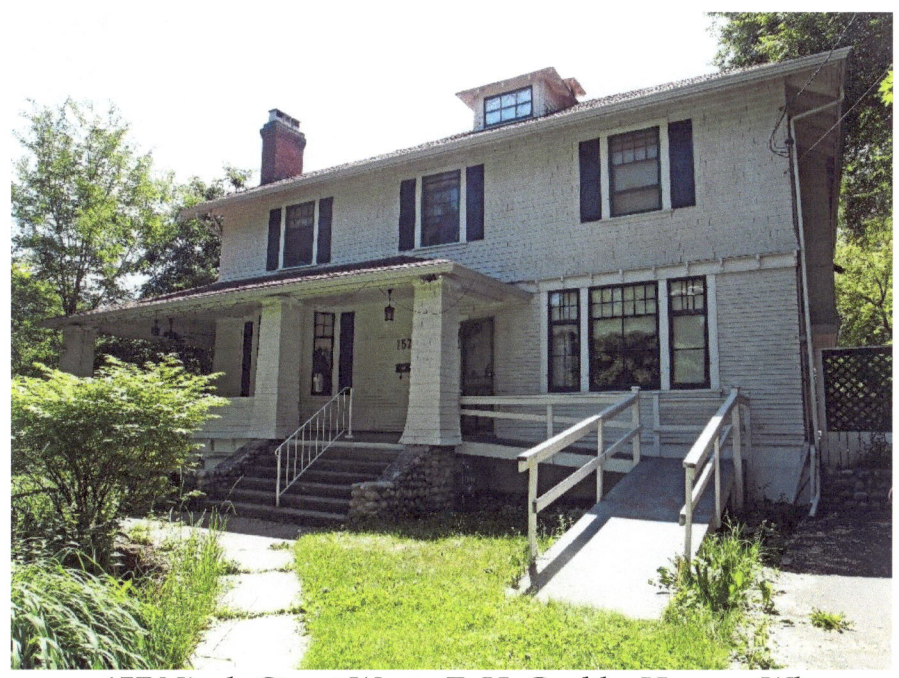

157 Nicola Street West –E. H. Grubbe House - When Eustace Grubbe built this house in 1912, it lay outside City limits and was surrounded by empty fields and was accessed by a dirt track. Grubbe was manager of the local Bank of Montreal.

    Architectural features of the house point to the Arts and Crafts tradition. The house has a wide front verandah with sturdy tapered columns, exposed rafter ends, and multi-paned windows.

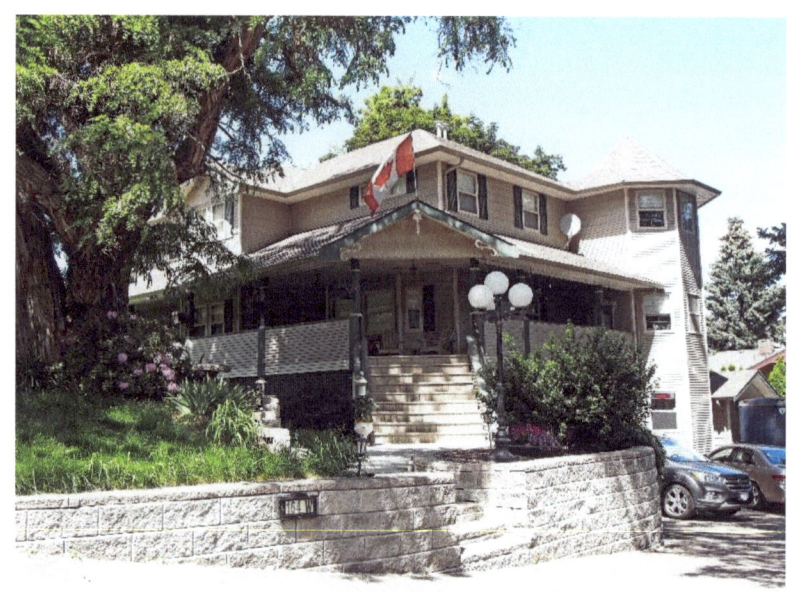

164 Nicola Street West

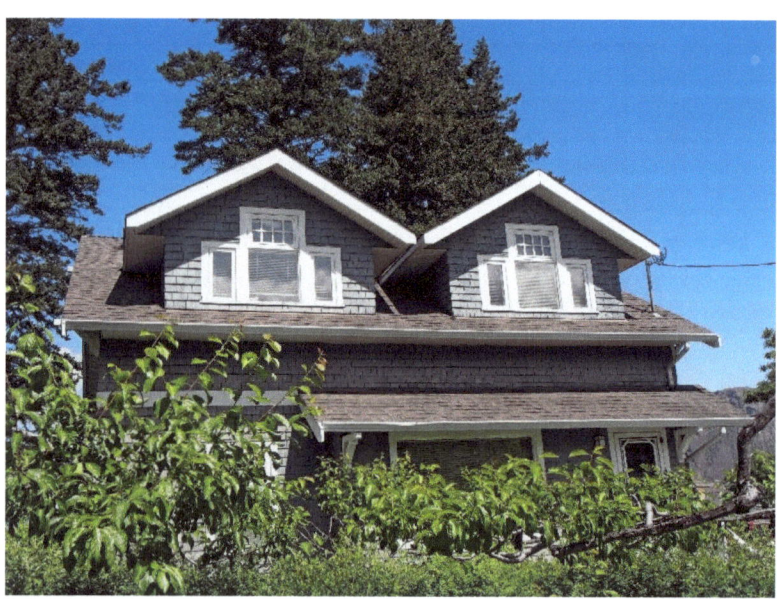

Nicola Street West – dormers with Palladian windows

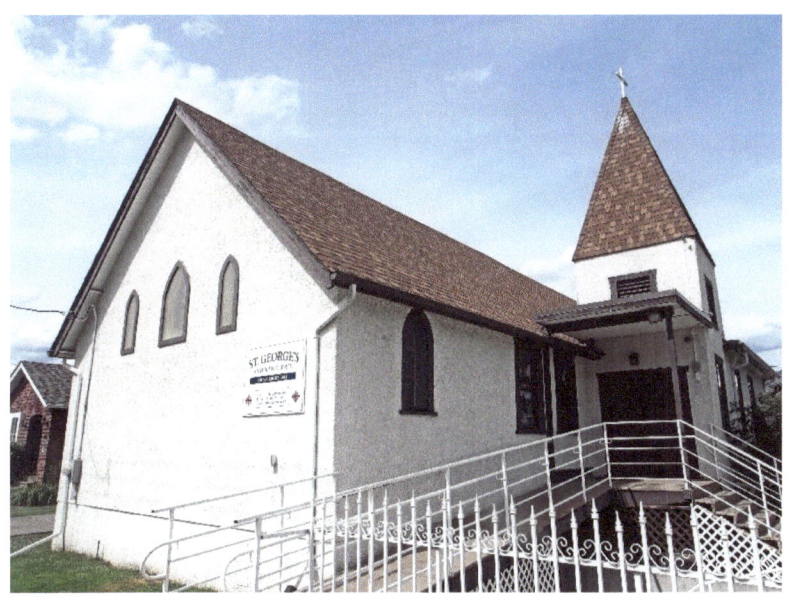

308 Royal Avenue – St. George's Anglican Church is the oldest church in North Kamloops and was built in 1927. Anglican worship in this area began around 1900 and early services were held in the BC Fruitlands' office and the local community hall.

In 1930, a lych gate arch from St. Peter's Church in Goose Lake, Knutsford was donated by Mr. Haverfield when that church closed. St. George's is the only church in Kamloops with a traditional British lych gate on site. The vicarage was built beside the church in 1938. This cottage, now named 'Shekinah' that translates as 'glory of divine presence' is now a place for parish meetings, offices and outreach.

After World War II approximately 1,700 Japanese Canadians came to North Kamloops and for many years, services were held for them at St. George's in Japanese. In 1966, the church was raised up and a basement added to create a larger parish hall for Sunday School classes and parish activities. The most notable feature of St. George's is its beautiful stained-glass windows.

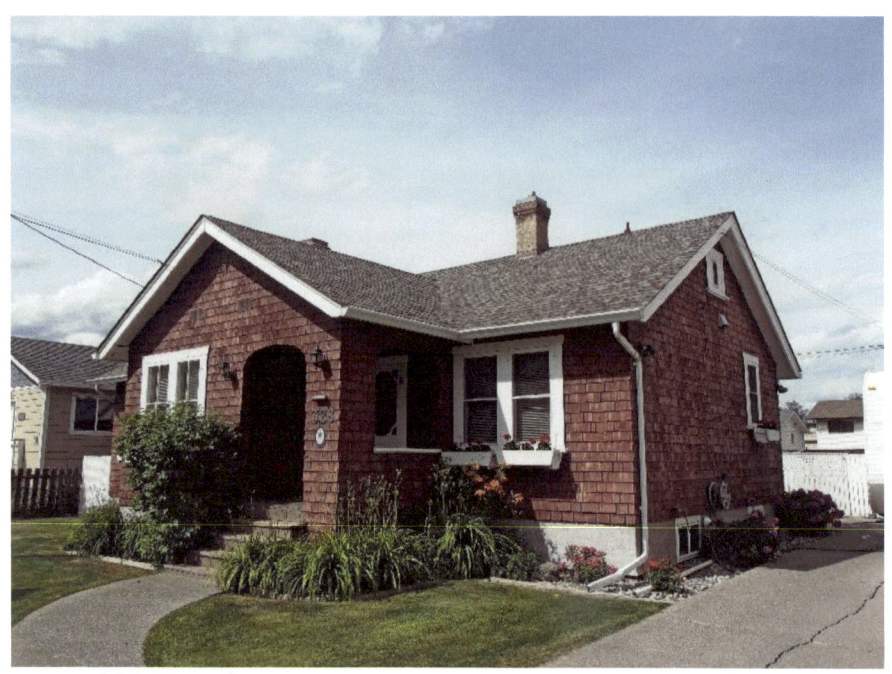

328 Royal Avenue – Tom Bones House - Built circa 1930, the Tom Bones House is valued for its association with the settlement of the North Shore of Kamloops. This was primarily a rural farming area with orchards and fields until 1909, when B.C. Fruitlands, a British-based company, was incorporated, and obtained over 9,000 acres on the North Shore. By 1920, the company had increased its holdings to over 22,000 acres, and installed an extensive irrigation system that supplied water to all of North Kamloops. After the irrigation system was installed, the company promoted programs to attract settlers to the area. Over time, the patchwork of farms developed into a community and in 1946, the village of North Kamloops was incorporated.

Thomas Bones, the first owner, was a local carpenter and his wife, Louisa Jane (née Fenner); both came from England. Tom Bones worked at the sanitarium in nearby Tranquille, and built this Arts and Crafts style cottage himself. His carpentry skills are evident on both the exterior and interior; the round stones for the fireplace were apparently collected from Tranquille.

Additionally, the Tom Bones House is valued as an example of an Arts and Crafts Period Revival cottage and is representative of traditional domestic ideals. Between the two World Wars, houses were expected to display some sort of historical reference in order to demonstrate the owner's good taste. An Arts and Crafts influence is demonstrated in the diagonally-cut window trim and built-in flower boxes.

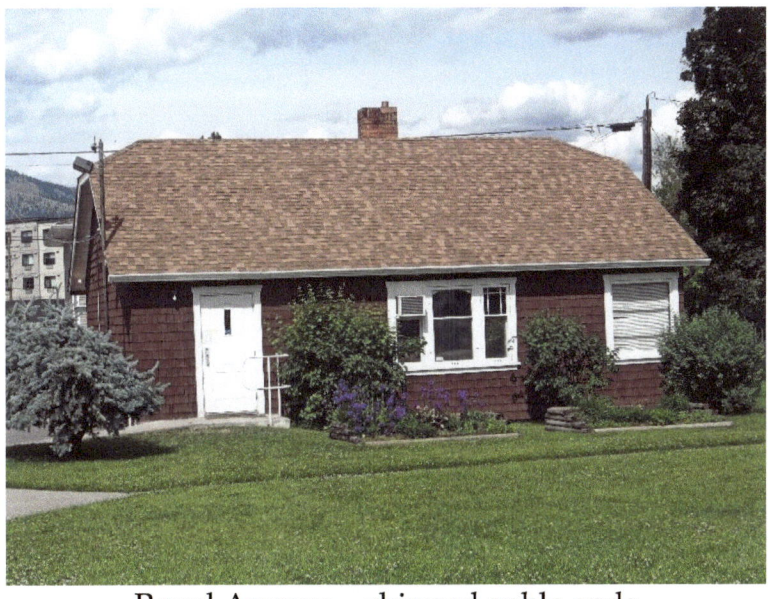

Royal Avenue – chipped gable ends

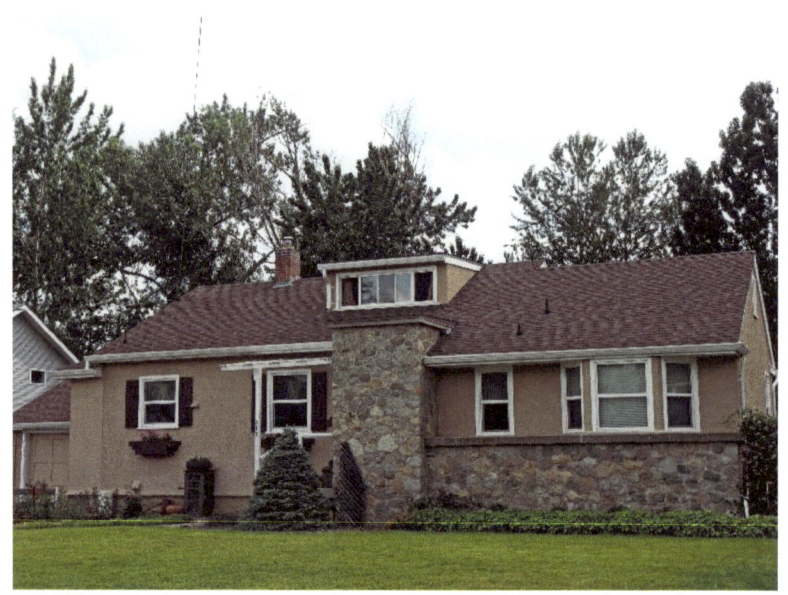

317 Royal Avenue – dormer, field stone foundation

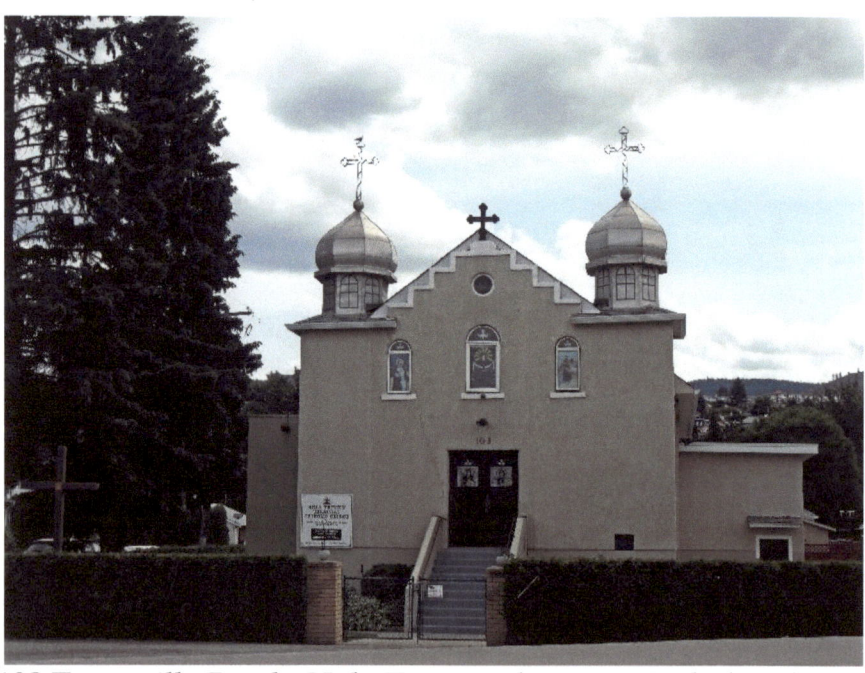

109 Tranquille Road - Holy Trinity Ukrainian Catholic Church – built 1951-1953

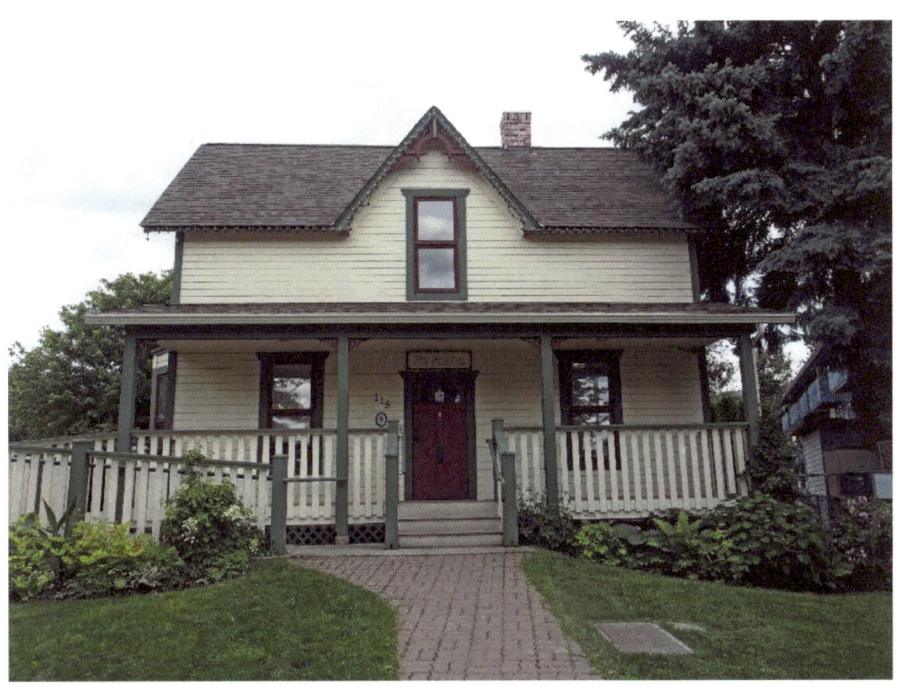

115 Tranquille Road – c. 1909-1910 - The Wilson House is a one-and-one-half-storey wood-frame house influenced by the Gothic Revival style and connected with William Stewart Wilson, a local farmer, businessman and politician, and the first Chairman of the Village of North Kamloops. The house has a steeply-pitched side gabled roof and side bay window, a central gabled wall dormer, and a full-width open veranda.

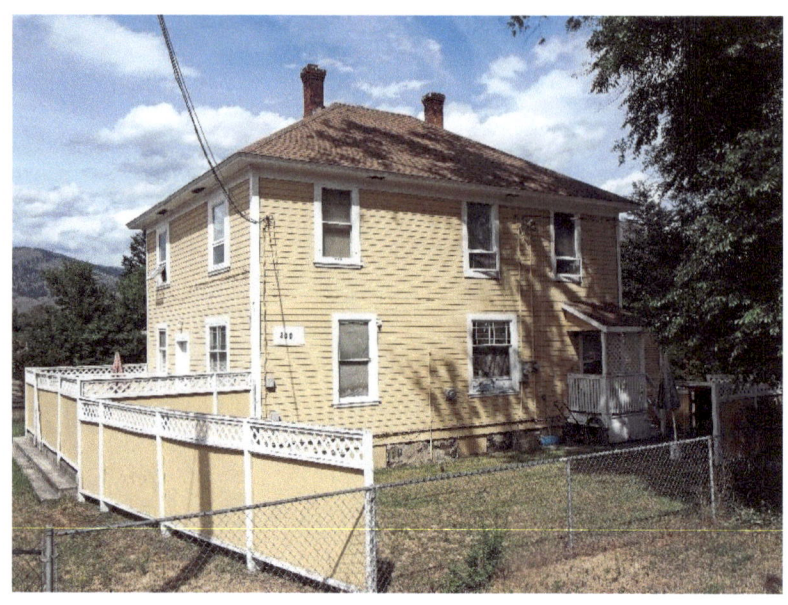

300 Fortune Drive – Fort House – built on Fort Kamloops land in 1907

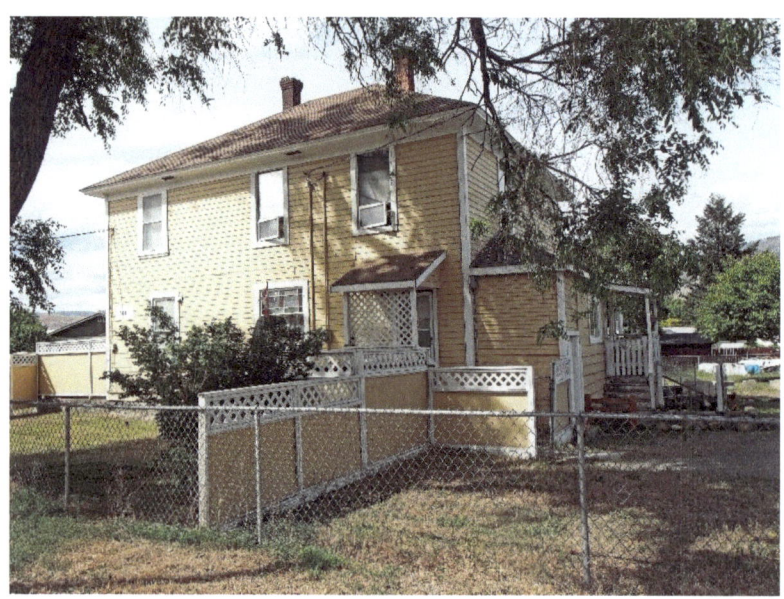

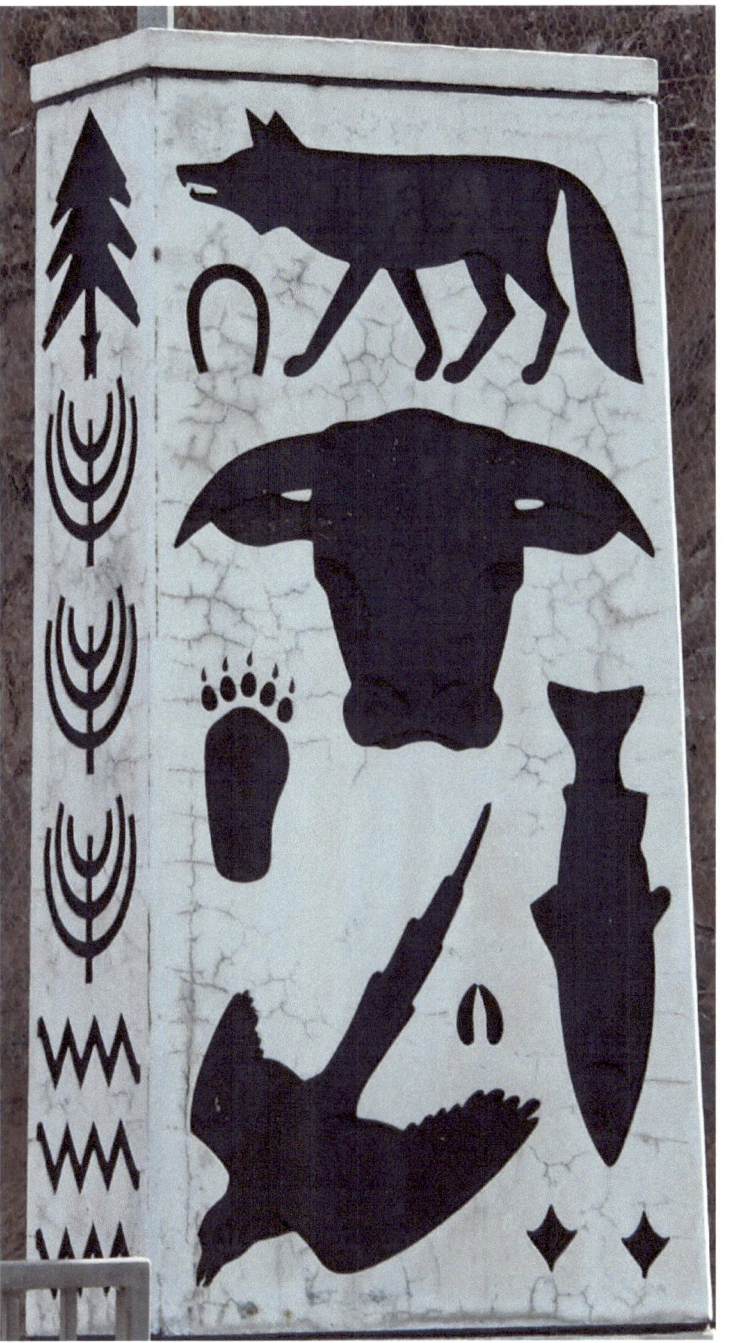

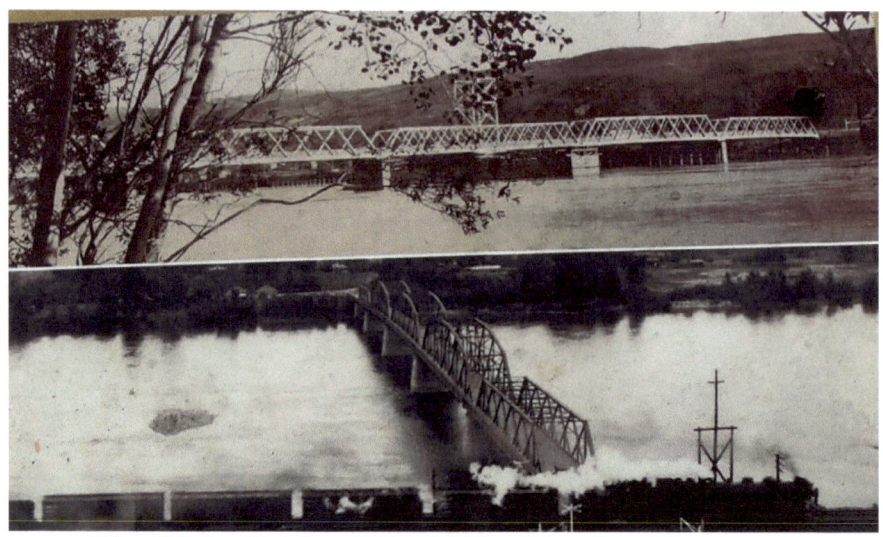

The White Bridge 1901-1925 – The first North Kamloops bridge was built in 1901 as a wooden swing bridge and was painted white. It was instrumental in opening up the North Shore's agricultural potential which allowed for the developed of the BC Fruitlands Company in the 1900s. A fire caused by sparks from the sternwheeler "Riffle" damaged the bridge and halted growth until it was repaired. It was condemned in 1923 and dismantled after 1925.

The Black Bridge (1925-1972) was the second West End Bridge and built with a black steel superstructure set on concrete piers. The bridge had two lanes, a sidewalk, and an inconvenient railway crossing at the south side.

The current Blue Bridge was designed to be wider to accommodate more traffic and avoid the railway crossing. It opened in 1961 and a year later during the centenary of the Overlanders arrival in Kamloops it was appropriately named the Overlanders Bridge.

Other Books by Barbara Raue

Coins of Gold
Arrows, Indians and Love
The Life and Times of Barbara
The Cromwell Family Book
Laura Secord Discovered
Daddy Where Are You?

Montana Series
Book 1: Montana Dream
Book 2: Life on the Montana Frontier
Book 3: Montana to Boston and Back
Book 4: Montana Sons Go to War
Book 5: Montana Sons Return from War

Book 1: Rite of Passage
Book 2: Rite of Marriage

© 2019 by Barbara Raue - All the photos in this book have been taken with my cameras. I own the rights to them.

Series Name: Cruising Ontario, Saving Our History One Photo at a Time in colour photos

Books Available in Alphabetical Order:
Aberfoyle, Acton, Ajax, Alton, Amherstburg, Ancaster, Arthur, Auburn, Aylmer, Ayr, Beaver Valley, Belfountain, Belgrave, Belleville, Bloomingdale, Blyth, Brantford, Brockville, Burford, Burgessville, Burlington, Caledon, Caledonia, Cambridge, Carlow, Cayuga, Chatsworth, Cheltenham, Clifford, Colborne, Collingwood, Conestogo, Delhi, Dorchester to Aylmer, Drayton, Drumbo, Dundas, Dunlop, Dunnville, Eden Mills, Elmira, Elora, Embro, Erin, Essex, Fergus, Fort Erie, Georgetown, Goderich, Grimsby, Guelph, Hagersville, Haldimand County, Hamilton, Hanover, Harriston, Hespeler, Ingersoll, Inglewood, Innerkip, Jarvis, Kingston, Kingsville, Kitchener, Lake Superior, Lincoln, Linwood, Listowel, London, Lucknow, Merrickville, Mono, Mount Brydges, Mount Forest, Mount Pleasant, Neustadt, New Hamburg, Newboro, Newport, Niagara-on-the-Lake, Niagara Falls, North Bay, Norwich, Oakville, Onondaga, Orangeville, Orillia, Oshawa, Otterville, Owen Sound, Palmerston, Paris, Parry Sound, Pelham, Perth, Peterborough, Petrolia, Pickering, Port Colborne, Port Elgin, Port Hope, Port Perry, Portland, Preston, Rockwood, Sarnia, Sault Ste. Marie, Seaforth, Sheffield, Shelburne, Simcoe, Smiths Falls, Smithville, Southampton, Southwest Oxford, St. Catharines, St. George, St. Jacobs, St. Marys, St. Thomas, Stoney Creek, Stouffville, Stratford, Strathroy, Sudbury, Tavistock, Terra Cotta, Thamesford, Thunder Bay, Tillsonburg, Toronto, Uxbridge, Waterdown, Waterford, Waterloo, Welland, Wellesley, West Flamborough, Westport, Whitby, Windsor, Wingham, Woodstock, York, Zorra

Book 238-239: Ingersoll
Book 240: Zorra Township
Book 241: Southwest Oxford
Book 242: Otterville, Burgessville
Book 243: Norwich
Book 244: Woodstock Book 4

www.ingramcontent.com/pod-product-compliance
Lightning Source LLC
Chambersburg PA
CBHW040234220526
45473CB00001B/236